Building the Dream

A self-build revolution

Jean Debney

Copyright © 2018 Jean Debney
All rights reserved.

ISBN: 9781980525660

The morale right of the author has been asserted.

Typeface set in Apple Baskerville

TABLE OF CONTENTS

Acknowledgements 6

A Foreword 7

Introduction 9

Part 1 - Four good walls and a roof 12

Chapter 1 - The Aftermath 13

Chapter 2 - The Town in the Country 22

Chapter 3 - Desperate times call for… 29

Chapter 4 - Fifty men of Brum 39

Part 2 - 'There hangs a tale' 47

Chapter 5 - From little acorns… 48

Chapter 6 - Laying the foundations 57

Chapter 7 - Brick by brick 73

Chapter 8 - And so, we build 83

Chapter 9 - Topping Out 93

Chapter 10 - All in the scheme of things 103

Part 3 - 'When needs drive' 113

Chapter 11 - Reflections of the past 114

Chapter 12 - St. Minver 123

Chapter 13 - Broadhempston 132

Bibliography 146

For Margaret and Joseph

Acknowledgements

There are number of people who have contributed to the compilation of my research, and the production of this book, that I wish to thank.

Without a doubt, all of the interviews that were conducted between the surviving members of the Silver Birch scheme and my brother James Debney have proved to be invaluable. The information, both oral and visual, that this group have willingly shared has given considerable detail to a story that was in danger of being lost and forgotten. I particularly wish to thank Reg and Dot Harvey, Harry and Joan Pestridge, Ken Quiney, Pat Rowson and Beryl Rose for their highly entertaining interviews. Others too who remain with us - Dan Ready and Rex Marfleet have provided further background information via my brother, who I also want to thank for his painstaking and careful facilitation of these interviews.

I am indebted to Solihull Central Library and Warwickshire County Records Office for making the past minutes of Solihull Urban District Council available for me to view.

My grateful thanks are also extended to Helen Rawe - Company Secretary to the St. Minver Community Land Trust Ltd., and to Gavin, one of the builders from Broadhempston Community Land Trust, for taking time out of their very busy lives to contribute exceptionally detailed accounts of the experiences of their particular Trusts. I know that they are continuing to work very hard to achieve their respective goals.

Finally, and by no small part, to my proof reader and friend Helen Davies, for helping to give sense to my dyslexic ramblings.

This book is dedicated to my parents Joseph and Margaret Debney who I know went through much personal sacrifice, to give our small family the opportunities that we have benefitted from. They inspired us all through their own determination, as I am sure each child from the Silver Birch scheme was likewise affected by their driven parents.

To all the community self-builders from the 'before' (1950's) and the 'now', I congratulate you for your tenacity and guts to give it a go, and I wish all those who are contemplating the adventure at this moment every success in your endeavours.

This is the hardest process that you are ever likely to undertake in your lives, but by far the most rewarding experience that you will ever have and the long-term rewards for you and your family will be without end.

A Foreword

SELF-HELP HOUSING ASSOCIATIONS
HC Deb 29 February 1952 vol 496 cc1674-84

Mr. Martin Lindsay *(Solihull)* *I hope this Adjournment period will be useful in giving an opportunity to the government to state their policy in regard to the numerous associations which are now springing up all over the country for the purpose of their members building their own homes. It happens that there are more self-help housing groups in my own constituency of Solihull than in any other. This is partly because the first of these associations, that of the Post Office workers, started in the neighbouring City of Birmingham, but chiefly because we are fortunate in having a progressive urban district Council, which believes in private enterprise, and enlightened officials. They appreciate that these groups of fine young workmen are performing valuable pioneering work, and have therefore given every possible encouragement to them.*

In consequence, we now have in Solihull no fewer than nine self-building groups in course of building, and several more which are in process of training and formation. There are some 100 of these associations in different parts of the

1675

country at the present time, but I am sure that the number will grow rapidly.

I believe, therefore, that the time has now come for the government to give considerably more thought to the housing contribution which these groups are capable of making and to the problems which they bring in their train. The most important of those problems is the question of relations with the trade unions if, as is likely, these groups grow to mammoth numbers in a few years. I trust the time will never come when there will be opposition to men building their own homes in a free country. Nevertheless, the relationship with the unions is something which must be considered in good time.

I want the Minister to realise, if he does not already, what an immensely valuable building potential these groups are at a time of great national labour shortage. In my constituency, I hope we shall complete 80 to 100 houses this year and about 150 in 1953. Taking this figure of 150 houses, if self-help groups would average only half this level of production all over the country, it would be equivalent to 47,000 houses a year—a bonus of 16 per cent. on the government target of 300,000 houses a year, without any call upon the normal building labour force.

I therefore believe that the government should do all they possibly can to assist well-managed building groups to come into existence all over the country. The housing need is there, the latent will to build is there, and what is required is technical assistance in the initial stages, such as guidance through the immense legal and administrative difficulties, which cannot possibly be envisaged by the ordinary man wishing to work in a group…

…It would be exceedingly difficult to find a movement more deserving of encouragement. What these men are doing is most impressive, working at weekends and in the long summer evenings, or, at the present time, by are lamps until 8 o'clock on Sunday nights. If the Minister could spare a weekend afternoon, there is nothing I should like more than to take

him round from one group to another in my constituency and let him see them actually on the job.

These are the men with guts and enterprise, who are getting on with the job instead of waiting for something to be done for them. Often they work a 78-hour week, whilst being paid for working 44 hours. I like to think that they are typical of what we hope are going to be the new Elizabethans.

(Hansard).

Introduction

As I am writing this introduction, the government of the day has just announced another strategy to try to address the crippling housing shortage that has perpetuated since the 1980's. The latest idea is to build garden towns and villages (not a new concept, as you will read later), and this is adding to the raft of proposed solutions of the past five years including: 'Right-to-Buy', 'Starter Homes', 'Self-build'… The list goes on and on; in fact, in the last six years, experts estimate that there have been some one hundred and eighty housing initiatives (Christine Whitehead, LSE). Still we fall far short of the required needs for house building and accessibility to those properties for the least well-off in society.

In 1981, one in three properties was a council house, or in today's jargon social housing. Now only one in ten houses is a social house; this is due to the selloff ('Right-to-buy') under Margaret Thatcher's government. Unfortunately, this depleted the stock while population and need rose; those factors combined with a global recession and a poor economic climate, have caused a stalling in investment by local Councils in their stock and a collapse in the building industry.

But is it possible to build on such an enormous scale when all of the odds are stacked against you? When the country is short of money? Land is at a premium? Materials and labour are in short supply? When money is tight for the man (or woman) in the street? Is this government trying to achieve the unachievable, or is there a historical precedent by which they can argue?

In this book, I will tell the story of the families in desperate need, whose determination and hard work enabled them to obtain homes. The government of the day took a keen interest, and by that effect, an active role in driving the necessary bureaucracy and red tape away, and directing financial help where it was needed.

At the end of World War II, the United Kingdom was facing a problem of monumental proportions, particularly in urban manufacturing cities, where Hitler's policy of blanket-bombing had been strategically targeted. These were the places that the working class lived, where Council accommodation and slums housed the many. Where the bombs, armaments and aircraft had been manufactured to support the war effort.

In one of my previous books, *The Dangerfields: Munitions and Memories*, I told the tale of Birmingham and the effort by the women of the time to fill the place of the men away fighting. I recounted the evidence from the National Archive of the Home Survey from the time, that painted a picture of constant waves of bombing, particularly in 1940, that led to a shattered city. Many were left homeless and dispossessed, and fires, out of control through lack of water, left a city unable to recover for the rest of the war. I return now to discuss the aftermath of the largest conflagration on British soil and how we recovered, despite crippling economic problems, added to by labour and material shortages.

I will tell you the story on several levels: a historical perspective of that time and the successive governments' response to the crisis of housing; the local demographic of two very different places, Birmingham and Solihull; and a personal tale, as I grew up in a house on the self-help scheme that is the subject of this book. My father, Joseph William Debney, was the treasurer and one of the trustees for the Silver Birch scheme, as well as a builder's labourer, so I have a more than passing interest in keeping this history alive. He and my mother lived in their home till the day that they died and I know he was enormously proud of what they had achieved.

Over the period of two and half years, twenty-eight men (and their wives of course), managed to build twenty-eight, semi-detached bungalows. This was while working in full-time employment, half with no previous experience in the building trade whatsoever, and half with very young children. All with the same determination to put a roof over the heads of their families, and prepared to undergo whatever hardships they faced during that monumental effort.

Although I do not claim it as the first scheme of its type, it may well have been the first to complete, and stimulated over forty schemes locally and in excess of three hundred and fifty nationwide. These schemes made considerable contributions to meeting the housing shortfall of the time and there is no doubt that without them many would have waited a long time before they lived in their own property. Some may well have never aspired to home-ownership and been subjected to the vagaries of the rental market for the rest of their lives.

From a personal point of view, my parents had five children, and I am sure that would not have happened, had they remained in rental accommodation. We had a home of our own; my father loved his garden and was the epitome of the phrase, 'an Englishman's home is his castle', for to him, it was. That view, I know, was shared by all of the twenty-seven other families in our scheme, and from the research this is a common theme for all other self-help schemes, as are the intertwining threads of determination and pride, both in the past and now.

I would like this book to celebrate the incredible undertaking of all those families nationally who managed to obtain self-help homes (many families still retain these). I would particularly like to celebrate the Solihull Urban District Council of the time, for its foresight and visionary planning, but most of all, the members of Silver Birch Housing Association. At the moment of writing this book, a small handful remain living and have contributed to my research: Mr Reg and Mrs Dot Harvey, Mrs Pat Rowson, Mr Ken Quiney and Mrs Beryl Rose. Sadly, we lost Mr. Harry Pestridge a few months before I started to write this book, his wife Joan remains in good health and I am sure this represents the national picture of only a handful left from many of these schemes.

This, like all of my history books, is very much about keeping the history alive, saving it before it dies and becomes hearsay. I must make due credit to my brother Mr James Debney, who first suggested this topic and has undertaken all of the interviews with the remaining survivors, and has subsequently set up a website (www.self-built.uk) to commemorate Silver Birch. We have both uncovered vast amounts of data and not all of it can be included in a book of this size. If you would like a further tour of the information gathered, please visit this website, and if you are the offspring of those involved in other schemes, we would like to hear from you and look forward to expanding the contact network.

I have been lucky to find some evidence in the National Archive, and in Warwickshire County Records Office, but by far the largest archive is that held by Solihull Library. I would like to extend my grateful thanks to Mrs Tracey Williams, who is the Heritage and Local Studies Librarian there, for allowing me to access the records. Solihull has every reason to be proud and stand by its achievements of helping poor struggling families from over the border at their time of greatest need.

In my opinion, a great deal can be learnt from the undertakings that are detailed in this book, especially in this time of housing shortages where incentive schemes and proposals are crowding the housing legislation. Yet, we fall far short of our current target of two hundred thousand affordable homes. It is time for someone, or some group, to re-examine the post-WWII self-help strategies, and to incentivise and encourage those with the need and desire to build their own homes. It is with that thought that I have divided this book into three sections. Part One, examines the 'why?' In other words, what were the circumstances, over a period of twenty years, that generated this desperate shortage and created the need, and also what legislation enabled this movement to act? In part two, it is the story of one of these movements, the Silver Birch Housing Association. I have included a chapter there, to pay tribute to three other associations in Solihull who have left a record of their achievements deposited at Solihull Central Library local history archive. Part three is a brief examination of some self-help (build) schemes of present-day. In this final section, I have gathered the stories of two of the many Community Land Trusts that have been established in the south west; generally, where houses prices and land prices have outstripped average disposable incomes substantially. In other words, necessity and desperation has driven individuals to come together to address their own housing needs, in much the same way as the acute housing shortages of the 1950's left my parents' generation no other choice than to do the same. At the present time, these Trusts are in pockets of activity, and subject to changes in government funding and attention, this means that when changes in government occur, they have a high profile and access to support and in the lean times, less so. What is interesting is how few people seem to be aware of this opportunity. Again, in the 1950's it took the words of Martin Lindsay MP to propel the concept into the national consciousness, and the fact that there is a perceived lack of general awareness now may be the reason why so few people attempt this undertaking, and further, that the hotspots of this kind of activity are most prominent in areas of extreme house prices and housing need.

The two CLTs, St. Minver in Cornwall and Broadhempston in Teignbridge, Devon, have been candid and frank about the hard work and determination that it has taken for them to complete their projects. Equally, they remain enthusiastic and euphoric about all that they have achieved. This is a mirror of the findings of those groups that were doing it for themselves seventy years ago; the self-help movement then was high profile, and involved thousands of people, now you can count the subscribers in the hundreds. In my opinion, this movement can happen again in strength, if the will within government is there to facilitate and assist in the finance of the 'build' process (that too needs to be de-mystified and made practical for those that might wish to attempt to do it for themselves). After all, it can be done, it was done, and it is still being done.

Part 1

Four good walls and a roof

Chapter 1

The Aftermath

"There'll be bluebirds over
The white cliffs of Dover
Tomorrow
Just you wait and see
There'll be love and laughter
And peace ever after
Tomorrow
When the world is free
The shepherd will tend his sheep
The valley will bloom again
And Johnny will go to sleep
In his own little room again"

Those famous lyrics immortalised in *White Cliffs of Dover* by Dame Vera Lynn in 1942, were the wish of all through the long dark years of the war. However, upon returning, the servicemen and women found a very different picture awaited. For some, it was a welcome homecoming, particularly for those that lived in the rural parts of the United Kingdom. For them, apart from resuming positions that had been filled in the intervening war years by the Land Girls and munition workers, the transition back to pre-war times was less fraught. Those that lived in the inner cities found many difficulties and complications in adjusting back to life prior to 1939. It is true to say the biggest challenge faced by many was just finding somewhere to live. In many cases 'Johnny' could not 'sleep in his own little room again' as it had been totally destroyed in the Blitz.

I stated in the introduction that it is important to place this story in the political and economic context of the time. It is only by asking why these people were so driven, determined and even desperate to build that we can understand what the circumstances are that could facilitate many more to make this attempt today. To do this we need to go back as far as the 1918 Housing Act, when the effects of housing shortages and inadequate housing were first catapulted to the top of the government agenda under Lloyd George. The campaign at the time 'Homes for Heroes', sought to address the shortages for many of the returning men who had served their country and found nowhere to live on coming home; many were injured with invisible mental scars as well as the more obvious physical problems (we call this Post Traumatic Stress Disorder today). The Liberal government pledged to build 500,000 houses in three years, but when the money ran out and the political will with it, they were only able to deliver 213,000.

This was not to say that this scheme ended then, for it continued through successive governments in the interwar years. Housing conditions of the time were appalling, with

1. The Aftermath

many in high-density, urban-industrial areas that were slum-ridden. It was a sad indictment on the centre of a dwindling empire that sought to keep itself as a world power, that its own people (many employed in the manufacturing centres providing substantial world exports) were housed in such dreadful conditions.

The back-to-backs in Birmingham are a prime example of the many thousands upon thousands of dwellings around the country that housed the poor workforce. These homes were one room deep, and comprised of three rooms. They were accessed from a communal courtyard, that also contained the privy (toilet) and washing facilities; these scant amenities were shared by fifteen other families. As one might imagine they were disease and vermin-ridden. These houses were perpetually damp and cold, and with such close proximity of living conditions mortality in every age group was high. The very poorest lived here: those that were only just avoiding the workhouse; those that were disabled, elderly and infirm; and the many that just did not earn enough to rise out of the poverty trap. Or indeed, needed to be close by their place of employment.

The 'Homes for Heroes' strategy was used to attempt slum-clearance. That would take another thirty years to near completion, as the first unpredictable factor occurred when, in 1939, Britain went to war again. Amazingly, 1,100,000 council houses were completed during the interwar years (that meant that 10% of the population were housed), compared to 3,500,000 private homes. However, David Kynaston writes in his book *'Austerity Britain 1945-51'* that 'despite a reasonably energetic slum-clearance programme' that:

> "About seven million dwellings lacked a hot water supply, some six million an inside WC, almost four million a fixed bath."

It was also estimated at the time that the programme to build had a significant shortfall of 500,000 houses from 1939, and the population had risen by nearly 1,000,000 by 1945. During the war, council house building was all but suspended (153,000 were completed that had been started in 1939), allowing the resources to be diverted to the war effort, although private building did continue at approximately 250,000 houses per year. But, of course, the Luftwaffe had a huge impact on housing during the Blitz of 1940 and 1944.

Figures vary depending on the source and whom they were written for (government, local authorities, archives). It is estimated that during the war 200,000 homes were completely destroyed, with 3,500,000 receiving significant damage. This equates to 2 in 7 homes overall. Of those, 450,000 council houses were completely destroyed or rendered uninhabitable. Allport notes in *'Demobbed'* that '60,000 million changes of address had taken place since 1939'. During the hostilities, some reparations to council houses were made; 103,000 were restored during the bombing, 1 ¾ million received 'first-aid' and a further 1 ¼ million received extensive repairs. Obviously, much of the concentration of the bombing was on inner city areas such as: London, Birmingham, Manchester and Glasgow and the docklands, as our munitions and aircraft production was centred in these areas. These places were the sites of greatest population density and the vast majority of the working class lived there. As such, the slum-clearance and council house placement had been concentrated in these areas. This meant that, by 1941, the numbers of homeless people in Britain were enormous; 1.4 million were declared homeless, and 7 million homes were not up to standard.

Some attempts were made by the war-time government to address emergency housing. Prefabricated bungalows (or Prefabs as Churchill called them) were small aluminium (in most cases) one-storey bungalows. They were self-contained units, with

1. The Aftermath

kitchens, bathrooms and heating. These were viewed as a very effective solution, and in 1944 Churchill's ambition was to provide 500,000 of these as emergency housing. There were logistical problems regarding manufacture (all factories were dedicated to the munitions efforts) and as consequence delivery of the finished units was slow. Local authorities continued to order them at the end of the war, but faced the same problem of extreme backlog. Additionally, they were only considered a temporary solution, with life expectancy of between ten to fifteen years; and as many of you are aware, there was still evidence of these houses in extensive use in and around Birmingham as late as the 1980's, far exceeding their maximum fifteen-year lifespan. Only 156,623 of these prefabs were built between 1945 and 1949.

The problems of persistent poverty and lack of care for the population added to a changed mind-set in the country that led the Labour's convincing victory under Attlee in 1945. The Labour Party had formed part of the war time coalition under Churchill, and had worked collaboratively with the other parties delivering the Total War Economy. In the second part of the war, when victory became a matter of time rather than the first half when we could be considered to be losing, they were active members of the plans for reconstruction post-war.

It is important to remember that a whole country had been mobilised in an all-consuming war effort. Class boundaries had all but dissolved; when you fought next to a man in uniform you did not stop to consider his class, and equally many women from middle and upper classes were mobilised to work in factories, field hospitals, or on the land. The 'Dunkirk Spirit' that is so often discussed was a shared mentality among everyone. Black-outs, air-raids, rationing, and bombing were the same for everyone no matter who they were or where they came from, and this meant that for the first time in British society everyone had a dialogue of a common and shared experience. Additionally, the British got used to working together and depending on one another, and more importantly, grew accustomed to all of the government rules and regulations that came thick and fast throughout the war years. We were used to taking orders and depending on the state for direction.

When Labour offered the Welfare State with 'Cradle to the Grave Care' as the mainstay of their manifesto, it was an appealing proposition and a natural progression towards a more egalitarian society. The benefits of free healthcare, pension provision for the elderly, state education for all allowing greater aspiration were the inspiration of the Beveridge report compiled in 1942 that shaped the Labour manifesto. Sir William Beveridge identified the 'five giants' of 'want' (poverty), 'squalor' (inadequate housing), 'disease' (ill health), 'ignorance' (lack of educational opportunity) and 'idleness' (unemployment). The keystone of that report was that better living conditions led to better health and life expectancy for the population as a whole, and greater productivity in the workforce, and was therefore of great benefit to the national economy. Houses had to be the main priority of any government coming into power in 1945. Churchill would have liked the coalition to remain for a few more years at the end of hostilities in Europe in 1945, but the Labour Conference on 21st May decided unanimously to breakup of the coalition and force a general election.

Clement Attlee promised to build a million homes in the term of that government; a promise that might have been achievable in peacetime, had it not followed a devastating world war, associated with a number of unforeseen circumstances that followed and conspired against that goal. Furthermore, Britain was still in the view that it was a leading world power and wished to continue in that dominant position, which was an expensive concept to facilitate. There was also an adherence to Keynesian economics, that insisted that state intervention in the economy should guarantee full employment. In other words, by the nationalisation of key industries such as coal, rail, steel and road haulage, everyone would pull together, and work productively. At the same time, wages could be kept low, thus guaranteeing full employment. However, you can only spend your way out of recession if your population has the wherewithal to buy things and if those 'things' are available in the first place. No one planned for 'Austerity'.

The first problem to undermine these great aspirations was the cancellation of the 'Lend-Lease' by the USA in 1945. Until 1941, the USA had refused to become embroiled it what it saw as a purely European conflict. Pearl Harbour changed all this and the Americans quickly realised that they needed British allies to wage a war against the Japanese in the Pacific. At that time, as I point out in my book *The Dangerfields: Munitions and Memories*, Britain had stood alone against Hitler as the rest of Europe fell under German occupation. We were all but finished economically, due to huge drain on our resources that had been required to arm and feed our forces, as well as the home population. The USA offered to lend resources and materials on a long-term lease basis to all of the allies; Britain had by far the largest share. It enabled us to keep up our pre-war profile of global dominance, on credit. When the decision was taken to end the lease, Britain was effectively bankrupt and had to beg the American government for a loan of £1,000,000 to buy food, raw materials and equipment; this was topped up a few years later by the Marshall Aid plan, again from the USA. The national debt of the UK in 1945 was substantial; our balance of payments was critical. Even if the materials, food and equipment were available (certainly very little was in war-torn Europe), it was at an extremely high cost, and too high for an insolvent country to afford.

Attlee appointed the charismatic Aneurin Bevan as Minister for Health in the new government; this was the key appointment and the bedrock of their Welfare State. As he covered all of the health brief, so too housing came under that brief. Some might argue, given hindsight, that this role was far too wide-reaching for any one department to achieve comprehensively. However, Nye Bevan was certainly not lacking in the determination of mind and opinion to take on the role. He was a socialist through and through, having come from a severely deprived part of Wales, and saw the problems in a holistic way. He believed emphatically that all the provisions of the Welfare State and Health Care should be free (a position that would lead to his eventual resignation on a point of principle and that would have severe repercussions for the government of the time).

Bevan set about the task of organising the house building strategy. As materials were in short supply, and were too expensive, and labour was in even shorter supply, all things had to be centrally controlled and rationed. This meant that the priorities for delivering the million homes needed had to be centred entirely on council house provision; private house building would not be a priority of this government. It is fair to say that, as is clear from the statistics given and the urgency of homing over one and half million people, that those in most need were in the middle of the cities that had been badly bombed. Those cities were where the much-needed manufacturing took place to be able to produce goods for sale and export, to get the country back on its feet. As such, urban areas got the largest share of those limited resources available and that had to be carefully apportioned.

Building licenses had first been introduced during the war under Defence Regulation

1. The Aftermath

56A. The Ministry controlled the allocation of these licences for each individual building 'start' and they were issued to authorities sparingly. This meant that materials and labour were spread out to accommodate all the sites of building and no one city (such as London or Birmingham) could take the lion share. London by far had the greatest number of homeless people - some estimates quote 1,000,000; Birmingham had in excess of 70,000 and Glasgow 40,000. However, it would be fair to say that, as the second city and having the greatest population of industrial workers per capita, Birmingham could have been re-built relatively quickly, if it had been left to its own devices to build and not restricted by central government.

That is of course if the workforce had been available. According to Stephen Merrett in his book *State Housing in Britain*, there was a considerable shortfall of trained manpower at the end of the war; again, a theme that affected every walk of life and made it impossible just to return to the 'business as usual' of the pre-war period. All resources had been diverted to the war effort in the war years, and, apart from those contracted to make emergency repairs (which divided the work force further), no training went on during that time; many had fallen as causalities during active service so there was a substantial reduction in the available trained manpower. Merrett states that in 1939 the workforce had exceeded 1,000,000; by 1945/46 it had fallen to 337,000 and 'despite rapid' demobilisation and training in 1947, the workforce was still only 200,000. This was 100,000 men less of the required manpower.

It is interesting to note that 4,000,000 servicemen were demobilised between 1945 to 1947; as Kynaston notes, this was 'too slow according to many'. Yet the majority of these returning men found that their jobs were not there when they returned. The promise to keep positions open was not always honoured for those back from the 'forgotten war' in the Far East, who had returned over a year after those demobilised from Europe. Of course, many of those late returnees could well have been the absent construction workers, but the job had to be done in those intervening two years and there just were not the men available there to do it.

I think it is also important to note at this time something that will become more apparent later in this book. Although building a house can be a relatively simple affair now, especially with the advent of quick-build technology and large prefabricated sections and units, you still need a certain amount of expertise when laying the foundations and a hard pad. You need expertise in plumbing and drainage, and you need qualified electricians. Then (without quick-build) you need to add carpenters, bricklayers and plasterers to the list. Anyone can labour; labourers are easy come by, but qualified trades are a must, and were more so then. This is where the problem started for building houses in number.

Material shortages were crippling. Houses at this stage required: concrete for foundations; ceramic bricks for walls; ceramic and concrete tiles for roofs; copper piping for water; ceramic piping for drainage; metal conduit for electrical (copper) wiring; gypsum for plastering; ceramic tiles for floors; and of course, timber, lots of it: window frames, door frames, beams, roof trusses, internal walls. It is easy to forget the sheer volume of houses that were expected. With 500,000 that had not been built pre-war to finish the slum-clearance, the substantial bomb-damage, and a rising population, 1,000,000 may not actually have been enough. When we consider that our current target for building over the next three years is only 200,000 and that is thought by many to be unachievable (even with quick-build technology and not following a world war), this whole building programme from 1945 to 1949 was gargantuan!

1. The Aftermath

Additionally, the whole of Europe had just been through a major conflagration, and though some European countries were, relatively speaking, unscathed by bombing, most had some substantial bomb damage and repairs to make, which Britain, still perceiving itself as a world power, felt obliged to assist with. In the case of Germany – which had suffered substantial bombing because of the RAF – it was absolutely necessary to help with the reconstruction (the mistake of the aftermath of the Great War of making the Germans suffer was still in common memory and inadvisable to repeat). This, of course, was not only a substantial drain and a diversion of materials that were already in critically short supply, for a country that had major reparations of its own to make, but also very demanding on an impoverished economy that was surviving on a loan from the USA.

Bricks, drainage pipes and tiles had to be made and fired in kilns, costing more man-hours and considerable fuel costs. Copper pipe and copper wire had to extruded in a high-heat process; aggregates for cement and concrete had to be quarried; and trees had to be cut, then processed into building planks in saw mills. When we consider all the processes involving human intervention to produce the materials needed build, and then realise that many of these processes where either very understaffed or lacked premises, it is not hard to see how the log-jam for materials-acquisition occurred. The only option the government had was to import. With an already critical balance-of-payments (with imports far exceeding exports) and an economy based on a USA loan, restrictions and controls had to be made, hence rationing of materials and the continuation of building licenses. All efforts had to be targeted at getting the working-class back to the factories, thus providing acceptable living conditions for the working class (those that would be instrumental in getting the economy back on its feet). Providing those working families with affordable, decent, rented housing, was considered essential to that process. Reconstruction of the major industrial centres became the government's first priority.

This is not to say that all the planning for reconstruction started in 1945, for we know that the coalition worked extensively on planning from 1941 onwards. This led to the passage of the many key pieces of legislation during that time, probably the most important being that of the Education Act of 1944 to provide free state education to everyone. The coalition realised that housing would have to be a major priority, and that substantial damage to urban centres such as Coventry and Birmingham would require comprehensive planning. Following the report authored by the committee led by lord Uthwart, the war-time coalition established the Ministry for Town and Country Planning in 1942.

When Nye Bevan took over as Minister for Health, assisted by Lewis Silken as Minister for Town and Country Planning, they instructed all Local Authorities to draw up a plan for house building, with everything controlled by the Ministry. As Murphy (1970) comments, Nye Bevan insisted that house purchases be discouraged. All council houses were to be rented, all private building had to be controlled by local authorities, but could not exceed one fifth of the government building programme. This was to ensure that the scant materials and labour force were prioritised towards the national programme. They introduced a raft of legislation to ensure that the vision for the 'new towns' could be enacted, but manpower was a persistent problem. Murphy notes that the industry as a whole was inefficient. Half of the 70,000 firms in the country were actually one-man operations; a third of the 70,000 had five or less employees and only 'one in a hundred had ninety-nine or more'.

We have to add to this that, while as a country we were dedicating all to Total War

1. The Aftermath

Economy, the necessary 'tooling-up' - and keeping abreast of technological advancement for manufacturing and construction - had been halted by the war. America had, however, continued to be a manufacturing economy throughout and had drastically improved their manufacturing and construction methods. Britain was still back in 1939, and though actual time had moved on by seven years, the country now had no money to invest in the equipment and vital new technologies it so desperately needed. Murphy notes that the average American could be fifty percent more productive in the same time frame. In terms of British house building he states that:

> "Before the war, one man working one year could complete a house, in 1945 three man-years were required for the same project."

He comments that low wages, lack of incentive, and job instability contributed to this lack of productivity. The government had only guaranteed employment for the life-time of the programme, which led to complacency. It also needs to be said that rationing led to poor nutrition and this was a major contributing factor.

The average soldier, before demobilisation, had dreamed of simple pleasures: returning to his own table, sitting by a fireside, good home-cooking. They had also eaten nutritiously as active servicemen; their diet was substantially better than that of the civilian population in order that they could do the job that was needed and fight. This is why rationing was introduced on the Homefront, and with Austerity, persisted for the term of the Attlee government. Once the soldiers returned and made the transition to civilian life, they had to adjust to the civilian diet, and then work in the many arduous physical occupations. Poor diet leads to lethargy and ill-heath; not the most auspicious of starts for the Welfare State and National Health Service.

These servicemen had been exposed to other cultures and societies far more than those soldiers returning from the Great War. They had received higher standards of education to enable them to conduct their war time occupations as pay clerks, radio operators, and engineers. Their personal aspirations and expectations were higher than those of their returning fathers and uncles. This is in part why the prefabs were not considered viable for these those men. They wanted and expected better housing; a more substantial and justifiable reward for their years of suffering and hardship. However, at the same time, they expected a pay commensurate with the tasks they were now undertaking to repair a shattered country.

Britain was in a mess; a set of circumstances had come together and conspired to cause delays and restrictions to the grand schemes of reconstruction first mooted during the war years. The idea of regenerating the economy through keeping all in full employment so that they would purchase goods and services and further boost the economic recovery was failing. This was probably unaffordable in the first-place due to low wages and, worse, very little was even available to buy. The balance-of-payments deficit was running out of control, with imports exceeding exports, yet not enough money was available to purchase the vital equipment and materials that we actually needed.

Everything had to remain apportioned and rationed. Ration books were still an essential prerequisite to enable purchase of food. The massive euphoria of 1945 that had occurred with the cessation of hostilities in Europe, and all the dreams and aspiration of the song made famous by Dame Vera Lynn, had disintegrated into a depression felt across the whole nation; we were in the time of 'Austerity'.

1. The Aftermath

With so many displaced and homeless, a large proportion ended up living with parents and relatives: married couples with children sharing one room, not just for months but for years. The lack of food, tiredness, and low energy levels felt by the many returning soldiers and civilians alike, meant that most failed to adjust to those years of post-war life as quickly as the government had hoped. This general malaise that gripped the nation had emerged through the combination of factors that collided at the same moment. Men had spent the best part of their formative adult lives involved in the active persecution of war as soldiers, or in the case of the civilian population, suffering constant air raids and bombing. As a consequence, mental health disorders rose dramatically. Serviceman found it impossible to be 'normal'; violence, crime, depression and suicide, became common-place. Nervous complaints were prevalent in those that had remained on the Homefront; post-traumatic stress disorder (in today's terminology) was a manifest part of society. The stress of then finding yourself living in cramped arrangements, or worse, having to squat in very sub-standard living conditions only added to the problems felt by many.

The visionary and valiant efforts of Aneurin Bevan to build 'new towns' of homes beneficial to the nation's health was meeting set-back after set-back. The Ministry for Health was requiring too much of his time elsewhere, as he worked towards establishing the jewel in the crown of the manifesto of the Welfare State. Further, the hardest winter on record between 1946 to 1947 led to electricity supplies being cut in order to conserve the much-needed energy for manufacturing. That, too had shortened days and weeks of production due to power-outages. The mammoth task of 1,000,000 homes seemed unreachable within the time frame. There were only 163,518 council houses started in 1946, with only 25,013 completed, as compared to 31,297 completed private houses in the same period. In 1947, 155,779 council houses were started, 97,340 were completed, and 40,980 private houses completed (Merrett, 1979). Given all of the problems that were encountered, with incredibly bad weather, a nation's finances shattered, the fact that over 190,000 houses were completed is quite astonishing, and something that today's planners should acknowledge in the light of current government initiatives.

Things had to improve, if only to address the persisting and enormous housing crisis, but with only three years remaining and luck not on the side of the government, how would it be possible to reconstruct a shattered Britain? By 1948, the national debt of the UK stood at two hundred and fifty per cent of the gross domestic product, the million pounds that had been loaned from the USA in 1946 was dwindling away rapidly. The USA had recognised that Europe's recovery could only happen if financial aid were given to those countries still struggling to make the adjustments back to peace. It was with that in mind that the Marshall Aid plan was formulated and substantial support injected into the UK, which had the largest share at 3.2 billion dollars. However, by 1949, although production had risen by twenty-five per cent, we were still importing far more than we were exporting. This led to a devaluation of the pound against the dollar by thirty percent in 1949.

The Attlee/Bevan vision of a million homes to rent was not making the huge targets necessary: in 1947, they had achieved 97,340 completions; in 1948, 190,368 completions; and in 1949 165,946 completions (approximately 100,000 private dwellings were completed over the same time frame, and that was with no access to private licences) (Merrett, 1979). Added to this, the General Election of 1950 was a dramatic downturn in fortunes for Labour. Having achieved a victory with a 145-seat majority in 1945, they were only able to get back

1. The Aftermath

into power with a 5-seat majority in 1950; and that was despite the introduction of the Welfare State and the raft of connected social reforms. People were tired and hungry, sick of austerity, many still homeless, and more were being added to those lists daily.

Unfortunately, King Edward VI had concerns that leaving for a Commonwealth tour with his government barely clinging onto power, and most of the Cabinet ageing and in poor health, was not good for the UK and asked for a second election to be held in 1951. By that stage, the political fortunes that had swung against Labour were to the benefit of the Conservative party. Labour called the election in a hope of increasing their majority, however, the Conservatives were returned to power under the leadership of Winston Churchill with Herbert Macmillan as his Minister of Housing with a majority of 17 seats. Macmillan set his targets higher, the Conservatives planned to build 300,000 houses a year. But despite an injection of capital resources from the USA, the problems were still the same; manpower and materials. How was it going to be possible to make this election pledge manifest without some very creative thinking?

It is in 1950 that the story that frames this book starts, when the main protagonist of the Silver Birch scheme first formulated his ideas to build his own home. As is clear from his narrative, his desire was built out of desperation for his own situation. In part two of this book the stories of Reg and Dot Harvey, Harry and Joan Pestridge, Ken Quiney, Beryl Rose and Pat Rowson (in their own words) will be told. It is important at this point to understand the impact of the end of the war and the advent of 'Austerity' had on the local environment and why Solihull became the central focus for those who, like the 'voices' in this book, decided that their only option was to build their homes themselves.

Chapter 2

The Town in the Country

This motto was the beginning of the first lesson that I ever had of our local Geography in the senior school that I attended in Solihull. Mrs Robertson, the Geography teacher, proudly informed us that Solihull (which was by then a Metropolitan Borough, having been a County Borough, Municipal Borough and Urban District Council prior to that), had a 'greenbelt'. She informed us that this 'greenbelt' was protected and not for development and that Solihull could proudly boast its Latin motto "Urbs in Rure".

In 1946 Solihull was an Urban District Council covering some 20,000 acres. Being centred around the picturesque High Street, with St Alphege church, the Manor House and Touchwood House, and a very good grammar school, it attracted those that wanted a more rural existence away from the city of Birmingham (Solihull MBC website). It began to evolve significantly with the arrival of the Rover Company in Lode Lane, prior to the Second World War. Land Rover Solihull, as it became, was used by the government during the war as a shadow factory for engine production; should the main factory be hit by bombing, the essential war-effort could always continue in Solihull. During war time, they produced the engines for the Hercules aircraft. This brought with it a larger workforce, mainly women. After the war, Rover wished to increase its operations in Solihull, and had a need to house a larger workforce that comprised of the many returning soldiers whose positions had been kept open, and the many new employees.

This proposed expansion was not just in the best interests of Rover, but had great potential for the economic growth of the town as a whole; more people working at 'The Rover' (as it became known), meant more money spent in the town and better for all of the local businesses. However, an increased workforce would need better roads, more schools, more shops and of course more houses. Solihull was in a tight predicament; not only had it not got the existing infrastructure to support this expansion, but it had been affected in many ways by the war, and its much larger neighbour Birmingham was encroaching on its undeveloped boarders with envious eyes.

It is estimated that Birmingham had over 70,000 people needing a home. The substantial damaged inflicted by the Luftwaffe in the war, with 77 air raids and 100 tons of bombs, had destroyed over 12,000 homes completely, and substantially damaged many more (Debney, 2011). It is true that, being the second city and an industrial area, it had a larger pool of available workers per square mile. If the materials and equipment had been obtainable at that time, the city would have had a far better chance of substantial reconstruction relatively quickly. However, as we have already considered, with the national economy in dire straits and materials in very short supply, Birmingham had to wait in the queue and take its rationed share of everything.

Birmingham was still slum-ridden. Despite the fact that slum clearance had taken

2. - The Town in the Country

place between the two wars, it was not enough to have made a difference, and the population had once again risen to just over 1,000,000. Even now it is known to be one of the most densely populated environments in Europe; it was considerably worse in 1945. Professor Carl Chinn has discussed in some length that, despite the efforts of the German bombardment, there were still 35,000 houses remaining that could not be considered habitable by modern standards (Chinn, 2015). Added to that, there were the many that had been made homeless by the Blitz. It is easy to see why Birmingham faced one of the greatest housing challenges outside London in 1946. It had the workforce - most probably many of those without homes - but it did not have the land on which to build. Even after the more densely-packed bomb sites were cleared they would never house as many people again in such a small area. With a risen population, and the need to expand industrial production, people had to be housed, not just for the good of Birmingham, but for the greater economic good of the country as a whole; the city had long had the reputation as 'the workshop of the world'. For Birmingham – and the much-needed industrial production for national economic regeneration – there was an urgent requirement to build much and quickly, not just the residential housing, but the new factories and business premises.

Solihull had land, plenty of it, and it sat just on the outskirts of this industrial metropolis. Solihull could become a victim of the same fate as the many outlying towns and villages that had been absorbed into the city's historical growth; King's Heath, Acock's Green, Yardley and Sutton Coldfield had all suffered similar land grabs, as the borders of the city reached further and further through its various expansions over time. Sheldon was at that time part of Solihull in the County of Warwickshire, as Yardley had been until Solihull had been changed from a Rural District Council to an Urban District Council. There was every reason to consider that Birmingham could once again make a very well-argued and reasonable claim to central government for its need for land to expand. The borders of Solihull were under threat, and Solihull UDC were conscious of this. Solihull needed to grow in its own right with urgency. It needed to expand its economic base to attract more people to move there, and to do that it had to settle and expand the local population substantially. Those in control in Solihull knew that they had to justify why they should not lose their undeveloped land to Birmingham.

And what were the common experiences felt by servicemen returning to Birmingham at the end of WWII? Most of those whose narratives form the main part of this book were from a slightly younger generation than my parents, who were the generation of returned adults of the time and shared many reflections of those first years immediately after the war. My parents' story was common to most of that generation who tried to resume normal life in post-war Birmingham.

My father, Joseph William Debney, was of the third generation of a family that had moved in from more rural parts of the Midlands at the turn of the nineteenth to twentieth centuries. The family had initially settled in the very inner quarters of the city, but the second generation began to move further out of the inner ring. My father had been a Saltley boy, having attended Saltley Grammar School and playing for their rugby team, before matriculation when, being good at maths, he started working for the Co-operative Society. His father had been an engineer at Saltley Gas Works (Nechells Power Station) and then later Chief engineer at Hams Hall Power Station. They were very much a local family and my father was in the Territorial Army before the outbreak of war in 1939. As was his patriotic

2. -The Town in the Country

duty, he walked the seven miles from Ward End where he lived then to the army recruitment office in the centre of the city, or the 'centre of town', as it was still known when I was young. Looking at the vast sprawl of the inner city now, it is hard to think that it was ever considered a town, and indeed, my father would not recognise it today. He did not recognise even it twenty years ago prior to his death. But he spent many hours reminiscing about the large swathes of rural land that used to exist on the outskirts of the city when he was a boy.

When I was a young child and he used to drive me around while doing his second job as supervisor for the 'Pools' (collections based on football results weekly – similar to the National Lottery today), we would visit many parts of the city collecting in the takings from the 'collectors'. Even then, we used to pass areas that had been vast sites of bombing, around Small Heath and Sparkhill, that had still not been redeveloped. He used to say in his droll manner that these were areas where they 'didn't want to find the bodies', meaning that there had been so many casualties unaccounted for during the Blitz that there may well be some still left in the piles of rubble that remained in the city. Certainly, this story was supported by some of the women that I interviewed for '*The Dangerfields: Munitions and Memories*' the bombing of the BSA (British Small Arms) factory being the prime example.

He used to reflect on all that had existed in his youth. He would tell me that Small Heath was the place to live with its Victorian villas and green spaces, as well as, Handsworth, Sparkhill, Sparkbrook, Greet and Tysley. We used to pass the Horsfall, Latch and Batchelor Factory at Hay Mills (where the Acker's Trust is now, and the BSA was before), and he would explain to me that the owner had built a church and accommodation there for his workers. This, we know, was common among the Quaker families that had settled in the non-conformist city, such as Cadbury when they created their 'garden villages'. I must admit, as a young child, I found it hard to visualise how these then run-down areas had been such places to dream of living in. As cities often go as they expand, the central areas become over-populated and those with money migrate to ever-growing outskirts and suburbs, leaving their previously owned homes vacated. Those that cannot afford to own houses then become tenants, and subsequently, these houses become grossly over-crowed with multiple lettings.

He was very proud of his city and when he met my mother in an air raid shelter 1940 and they married (probably with haste, as many a war-time romance did), it was the natural conclusion to stay there. My mother had no ties; if you have read another of my books (*Far Away Hills*) you will know that she had had her own dramatic start in life (born on a Canadian prairie in 1919 and promptly orphaned and shipped to Dunoon in Scotland), and had ended up in Birmingham after being bombed out of Leicester and London, where she had worked as a secretary. Having no family to speak of, and no physical anchors anywhere else in the world, and being of the generation where you complied with the wishes of your husband, she remained in Birmingham. After they married and she fell pregnant with her first child, she lived with my grandparents and their younger daughter in the family home.

This was a common situation in Birmingham both in war time and peace. Young people often remained with their parents, for a short while at least, when they were newly married. What became an unusual mark of this post-war time was the very extended periods that most now had to suffer these indignities and lack of privacy for. As it was war time when my mother and father met and married, she shared his younger sister's bed; a situation that my aunt was none too pleased with, especially as she had been used to her own space. My mother had my sister Dinah Patricia in 1944. Unfortunately, she succumbed to an infant gastroenteritis, and because all of the penicillin was on the front lines, reserved for the troops, she failed to thrive and tragically died. My father had been in the Royal Artillery, first as gunner, then a bombardier and very quickly made the rank of Warrant Office First Class. He had his share of movement; India, Africa and eventually Burma. As such he was not demobbed in 1945; it was not until 1946 he finally came home.

He was lucky that his job at the Co-op remained open and with the advent of the new Welfare State was going to form part of the infant National Health Service. His first position after this was to work as the financial officer at the Highcroft Hall Mental Hospital. Possibly because of that, and because he was in a slightly better position than most, he was able to rent a flat in Bromford Lane in Birmingham. That probably summons up visions of a leafy suburban lane or street to you; how often a name can disguise the reality of the situation. From the 1920 aerial surveys of Fort Dunlop Rubber Factory at that time, Bromford Lane was relatively leafy and rural, but by 1937 the Birmingham conurbation had begun to sprawl outwards and absorb the area; by 1947 it was a very built-up industrial and residential area.

My parents used to point the flat out to me whenever we passed it, on the major four-lane highway that the street had become. It was a very unassuming, small semi-detached house, built during the interwar years. It had black window frames, as I remember, and looked out onto this major road. They had the ground floor flat, and for a while a cat called Teddy. By 1947 my brother James was on the way. How they had faired that previous horrendous winter, or whether they had been affected then by the river Team rising and flooding I have no idea. Obviously, on my father's modest income they could afford the rent, that was not the same in many cases.

There were a very large number of families who had nowhere to go. The housing list was enormous, comprising of all those desperate families waiting for one of the promised council houses; those that found that their brothers and sisters had taken the only available rooms in their parents' houses; those that could not raise the income to pay ridiculous 'key money' to unscrupulous landlords, who were left with no alternative but to squat, and even squatting for some was better than the squats experienced by others.

In *'The Dangerfields: Munitions and Memories'*, I told of Daisy's story. She had worked at Kynoch's during the war, and found herself married, homeless, jobless and pregnant at the end of the war. She had no alternative but to squat in the Nissan huts in Perry Park, which had been a POW camp. She was pregnant in 1947, living in a hut that had no toilet facilities and a half mile walk to main gate to catch a bus.

Every disused army base, every POW camp, every disused ARP station was squatted. Some were fortunate and had electricity; many did not. Running water could also be a problem and toilet facilities lacking. The police and others turned a compassionate 'blind-eye' to their dreadful situation, knowing that the 'poor blighters' had no choice. Many of the police and authorities had probably served with these 'comrades' who now found themselves homeless, while their police 'friends' were prioritised for housing. Those that found themselves lucky must have been consumed with guilt for all those struggling, especially during that dreadful winter of 1946 to 1947.

Despite various rent controls established to limit rent paid on places to-let and furnished rooms, some landlords knew that the severe housing shortage was for them 'a licence to print money'. Although they could not demand a rent above a certain rate, they may well place an item of furniture that they wished payment for; the term 'key money' was

2. -The Town in the Country

used. In many cases these extraneous costs were just too much for some, and finding a place to take over illegally was the only choice left open to them.

The change from the Total War Economy to peace was not an overnight task. Many infrastructural changes had been made to local environments to enable the war and support it; all of those systems needed to be dismantled and that would take time. All normal Council business that would have taken place during 1939 to 1945, such as road and highway repairs and street lighting had been suspended, and much more disrepair was now felt because of the lack of general on-going maintenance. In Solihull, the infrastructural problems of trying to rebuild were manifest even in the Council itself, where a number of officers and surveyors had become casualties of the hostilities. This meant that even the task of trying to make a full assessment of the district in order to make a plan was proving difficult, due to the lack of officers available in 1946. Work that had been started prior to 1939, had effectively stopped for seven years, leaving roads unadopted (unnamed) and development suspended. It is clear from the Solihull UDC minutes from 1946 to 1947 (Minute Book/CR1577/Warwickshire County Records Office) for the Establishment Committee that there was a long way to go to get things back to anything near normal. They stipulated amongst their priorities an urgent need to house their own staff.

The Education system was a mess, and the demands of the Education Act that had been passed in 1944 would require a priority placed against the provision for state education. All of the allotment areas and recreation grounds had been requisitioned for essential food production; a situation that would endure for some time to come. There were British Restaurants in operation, in Solihull, Olton and Shirley; the food canteens of the war years, where everyone could get a reasonable meal at a reasonable cost; these would not close until June 1946. It was obvious that all departments of the Council wanted and needed something doing at the same time; all demands of each department were critical and the government's insistence to deliver the houses just added to the enormous pressures felt. This meant that painful decisions had to be made by some on the Council; lists of priorities had to be drawn up and adhered to.

The demands of the Midland Regional programme to build council houses in a year (based on the government's national programme of 240,000 for the country as a whole) was in excess of 20,000 houses; the Zonal programme was in excess of 5,000 houses. Solihull was tasked in 1946 with delivering 1,500 council houses over five years, but the national restrictions on supply and demand for labour and materials meant that all the associated problems of having to deliver these targets were compounded by the existing infrastructural problems nationwide. The government stuck to its mandate that all efforts should be directed to the building of the council houses and that licences that had already been issued prior to the war should now be restricted; civil and private building was to be rationed accordingly. Solihull assessed their land availability, of which they had plenty, many areas already had laid roads and services towards Cranmore Boulevard and Redlands Road in Shirley. It withdrew many private licences and restricted private building to 350 houses and 21 developers; this would mean that government's insistence of a ratio of 4:1 council houses to private houses might be deliverable (8/7/46 Housing Committee).

However, many roads and footpaths lay in a bad state of disrepair. Some street lighting was in need of attention or had never been installed. All of this required workers and materials and had to form part of the plan alongside national demands. It was decided to prioritise those problems that were considered a danger to 'life and limb' (8/7/46 Public Works Committee), as well as making efforts to survey and adopt those roads that lay unnamed, in order to assess what land and opportunity lay available to address their housing needs. The Housing Committee's assessment at the time stipulated that they required 3,000 houses (excluding temporary housing), double the amount of licences that they had been allowed by the government. How then could they deliver this need if the restrictions on licences meant that they could not be privately developed?

Squatting in Solihull was presenting difficulties for the Council. Homeless families had taken over disused military sites in Lode Lane, Haslucks Green Road and Hockley Heath Aerodrome and by November 1946, they were 'agitating' for better conditions; hardly surprising with the oncoming winter that followed. By December, the Housing Committee had agreed to improve conditions there but would charge rent to the occupants 7/6d per family. Meanwhile, the Council architect would make an assessment of exactly what was needed in five locations: Shakespeare Manor Estate, Dorridge, Hockley Heath, Robin Hood and Elmdon. However, the Council made it clear that any electricity supply was from the Birmingham Electric Supply Department and that the squatters would have to make their own arrangements. It is hard to imagine how dire the circumstances of living in these squats were during these dark and very cold times, especially as it is obvious that many did not even have electricity to light their squats, never mind keep warm (Minute Book/CR1577).

Meanwhile, Solihull was exploring all avenues of possibility for trying to increase the housing programme locally, in order to address the shortfall in licences and the needs that they had. They were in discussions with the local representatives from the Ministry of Health and the central Ministry itself, to see if any exceptions could be made, for instance the authority paying to build on its own land. Responses stated that, as long as it did not interfere with the labour and material supply for the main programme, all things were possible (5/3/47 Housing Committee).

At this point, Rover were lobbying the Council for assistance in housing its workers. The Council agreed with Rover that it should form its own Housing Association and set it up as a 'not-for-profit' organisation, with a plan to build homes for its workers based on their social class (adopting the same points system for gauging priority of need of its employees, as was being applied to all national council housing programmes) (2/4/47 Housing Committee). However, Rover had desires to expand and their housing needs were substantial. The proposed Housing Association would mean that they could apply for some of the licences being made available to the authority by the government, which the authority was unable to commence due to lack of materials and labour; there was a particular shortage of timber nationally that was causing great difficulties to the programme as a whole. Rover were not entirely happy with the proposition as, despite a grant per house being available to housing associations from the government, it would still mean a financial investment for the company, at a time when it wished to use that money for business expansion. Further, it would only meet a small proportion of its needs. Rover had to find other ways of producing the much-needed 300 or so houses for its workforce. The Ideal Benefit Society had been building in the area and Rover managed to secure a substantial number of those (2/7/47 Housing Committee). By 1947, the Ministry had suggested that it had 100 of the aluminium bungalows that would be available for the workers of Rover, and the Council began placing these on Damson Lane, but production and supply problems mixed with issues of quality

2. -The Town in the Country

meant that only just over 30 were ever sited there (10/9/47 Housing Committee).

By mid 1947, the government's housing programme was falling into difficulties. The original plan to have 600,000 houses started nationally by that stage, and have 300,000 completed (with 200,000 under construction and 100,000 in tender), was far short of its target. By that date in 1947, only 218,783 were under construction and 130,520 were approved but not yet under construction. Birmingham had completed just over 3,500 council houses and Solihull in excess of 350. The supply and demand of labour and materials was causing a log-jam, and the government decided to reduce the number of new approvals in order to catch up. Although the Zonal programme, particularly Solihull, was achieving the target set, it was necessary to restrict further new approvals. The government national figure of 240,000 to be completed before the end of that year, had to be restricted to the more realistic figure of 218,783 (4/6/47 Housing Committee).

Those authorities that had managed to address the exacting expectations of the government would now have to stall their programmes to enable the rest of the country to catch up. At the same time, yet another generation had housing needs. Those who were now returning from National Service did not qualify at all for the points system on the ever-lengthening housing lists. Many of these men were not in occupations that were seen as a priority to house, or they were builders themselves employed on the massive rebuilding campaign, yet unable to qualify as the future occupants of the houses that they were building. These were men like Reg Harvey, Harry Pestridge, and Ken Quiney and many more who worked for companies in Birmingham.

Solihull was caught in a bind of needing houses, not only for its existing population, but also for its rapidly expanding industrial population and at the same time be able to grow its own local economy to facilitate further expansion. By 1950, the population of Solihull had risen by over one-fifth since 1939, and was standing at approximately 68,000, yet it was still part of the County Borough of Warwickshire. If it could achieve a Charter of Incorporation as a Municipal Borough, it could devolve from county control (and any payment/taxes to the county), being able to secure such services as its own police force, and direct its funding into development of the municipal authority alone. There is evident from the minutes of the General Purposes Committee (2nd May 1950), that Solihull had been and was actively seeking to become incorporated; all attempts at that stage were being thwarted by the national review of local government that was on-going. Additionally, Solihull was still in the stranglehold of the 1:4 ratio of private to council licences that was restricting its further expansion, yet demands to house its existing and new workforce were even greater. It was at that time that the infant housing associations formed in Birmingham and began to make enquiries of the Birmingham City Council and Solihull UDC to build under the notion of Self-Help

All the circumstances that I have laid out in these preceding two chapters: the war itself, the fate of the economy, the Labour plans for a Welfare State, combined with shortages of monumental proportions and a terrible winter, led to the rise of a movement of those, who through necessity, were prepared to take actions to house themselves. In the next chapter, we will look at the genesis of the concept of self-help from the reports being made by government at the end of the war, and the existing housing legislation that had been enacted in the interwar years. In part two of this book that follows, we will explore, in the words of those people who remain to tell the tale, how they made the concept of self-help work for them and translated the legislation into action. Much is re-told through interviews relayed to my

2. -The Town in the Country

brother (he has pertinent thoughts too, as he was a young child at that time), much more survives through the traces and documents that remain.

Chapter 3

Desperate times call for…

As the phrase goes, 'desperate times call for desperate measures', and there hangs an air of desperation around each of the various 'emergency' solutions that were proposed to problems of reconstruction after World War II, although each of these 'solutions' were circumscribed with some strategic planning. The modern word I search for is 'spin': so often heard when the 'powers that be' wish to make a negative situation appear to be a positive one, as was the case of the 'prefab' solution to emergency housing.

It was in 1944 when the housing crisis was beginning to present severe difficulties to the coalition government that the solutions of quick-build were first explored. A number of prefabricated solutions were investigated and other solutions designed, in order to address the need for temporary emergency housing. Following the Burt Committee findings in 1944, Winston Churchill made a broadcast on the BBC to announce that the first priority should be to repair bomb damaged houses and that:

> "…The second attack on the housing problem will be made by what are called the prefabricated, or emergency houses… Factories have been assigned, the necessary set-up is being made ready, materials are being ear-marked as far as possible…"

In that speech, he announced his ambition that half a million of these 'prefabs' should be manufactured.

The first prototype, the Portal bungalow, had been exhibited at the Tate Gallery a year before the end of the war, with three other prototype designs. The minimum floor space for a prefab had been prescribed as 635 square feet. It had to contain a number of modern conveniences to make the concept attractive and appealing to potential residents: a prefabricated kitchen, with a back-to-back bathroom with integrated WC, a boiler and a coal fire. It was necessary to have multiple solutions to the prefab design, as no one manufacturer had the capacity of manpower or equipment, or the essential time for production. As such, each solution reflected the skills within that particular workforce; the accessibility of available materials and resources; and the plant and equipment available within that factory. All of the designs that were to be produced in order to achieve the target were agreed. Subsequently, a Housing Act was passed that stipulated each unit, regardless of manufacturer, should be internally decorated with magnolia walls and green gloss woodwork.

The prefabs were made in different configurations of materials. The original Portal bungalow had been manufactured with a steel frame, but as steel was in short supply because of the war, other solutions had to be found using: concrete, asbestos-cement, steel (limited), wood and aluminium. No one component could exceed seven and half feet in width for ease of transportation. One enterprising solution even used left-over aircraft components bolted together. The 'heart-unit' of the toilet and the kitchen adjacent was in order to limit pipework; only the American import did not have this as part of their specification. With the

3. Desperate times call for…

American Lend-Lease in place, a guaranteed supply of materials from the USA was being made available, and with the further promise of 30,000 of their concrete prefabs, it appeared at first that this might help to bridge the gap.

We have to remember that most people who would inhabit these prefabs had never known such modern conveniences as their own flushing toilet even external to their house, for in the back-to-back houses WC's had been shared by fourteen other families, as well as washing facilities. To have a toilet inside and of your own, with a bathroom, and a fitted kitchen was considered ultra-modern. Prefabs were very small – and before some became centrally heated much later – in the winter very cold at night, with condensation running down the inside of the walls and freezing. For many inhabitants, however, it was a luxurious home after knowing severe hardship. This is much of the reason why the ones that remain are listed and much-loved. The temporary solution that was meant to only have a life expectancy of 10 to 15 years has lasted much longer. The Phoenix prefabs on Wake Green Road, Birmingham, are a fine example of listed status; now enduring and loved for seventy years.

So why did the programme not deliver the success that it had first promised? And why were only 156,623 ever completed, a third of Winston Churchill's vision?

It was the abrupt ending of the much relied-on Lend-Lease on August 17th 1945 and the economic crisis that followed, that curtailed the temporary housing programme. Some would also argue that others saw these homes as unfitting for the fighting men returning, however many families did enjoy them. Cabinet papers from 1945 outline the problem that the government was faced with; it appears that the end of the Lend-Lease created an understandable panic amongst officials. The original budget forecast for the production of 500,000 houses had been estimated at £150,000,000; by October 1945 it became clear that this number of houses at the proposed cost was just not deliverable. Not only had the individual estimate per house at £600 been drastically underestimated, but material shortages and manpower shortages further escalated the costs.

The Lend-Lease had been a conduit for materials and the houses to be purchased from the American government that had in turn carried large subsidies that were now removed. In most cases the individual cost per unit was set to rise by one-third. A revision of expectations had to be made, and the whole project downsized to compensate for the shortfall in materials, manpower and funding available. The draft of the White Paper was laid out before the Cabinet (C.P. (45) 226) by the Ministry of Works on 13th October 1945. In it is a clear progression of the project, as envisaged from the previous optimistic views in October when the Temporary Accommodation Act had been passed. From the problems of proceeding with the original steel – Portal – bungalow (because of the need to conserve steel for munitions production), to the escalating cost of production (particularly in reference to the aluminium bungalow), that was set to rise in March 1945 to £900 per unit.

Following the demise of the Lend-Lease it had been realised that the expected 30,000 houses from the USA had to be drastically reduced to 8,000, as the costs of importation had risen dramatically from £800 to £1,330 per unit with the inclusion of £210 in custom duty, as well as rising costs of purchase without subsidy. By the time the draft White Paper had been put before the Cabinet, there was an average of a 30% increase in costs, with exception of the aluminium bungalow, that had now risen to an estimated £1,365 per unit. The briefing paper outlined that manufacturers had been over-optimistic in their original estimates of man-hours for the production of each unit. Additionally, the location where units would have to be erected in order to accommodate the factory population were inner-city areas, not the outskirts as originally proposed. Many of these sites were heavily bomb-damaged, and site-clearance, preparation and time would have to factored in to the costs to reflect this.

The end of the Lend-Lease impacted on this scheme substantially. Although it was only envisaged to buy 30,000 subsidised units from the USA, out of the original 500,000 proposed, the general supply of materials and resources from that country had been critical to the war effort. The immediate cessation of this arrangement limited the purchase of these units to 8,000, at a significantly raised cost, and the material supply-line (to assist the building of the remainder) effectively ceased. Those materials that were available from the UK or from Europe came at a very high premium, and also had to be directed toward the national house building programme as the first priority. Thus, severe rationing caused even greater difficulties to manufactures. From the draft White Paper, it is clear that, as early as October 1945, the government had decided to limit the Temporary Housing programme substantially to 158,480 houses at a revised cost (proposed) of £185,148,920. As we know, the final tally was 156,623.

There seems to have been a strange relationship with the prefab. Those that lived in them loved them dearly, and this is in part the reason why so many are preserved and listed. To others who viewed them from the outside, they were considered an eyesore, and the sooner they came to the end of their lives and could be demolished, the better. Whatever the personal relationship that was had with these little 'tin boxes', as some unflatteringly called them, the programme had to be ended due to a lack of resources and money in general, and a need to prioritise bricks and mortar.

The other major factor for the birth of the self-help movement in the 1950's is a section of legislation passed fourteen years earlier. The Housing Act of 1936 was one of the many interwar projects that combined the social attitudes of the time with the desire to remove the working families from the shambolic poverty that they existed in. As I have discussed earlier, this was a time of slum-clearance and despite massive recession there remained an imperative to improve the 'lot of the working man'. The council house concept had come into its own, and was seen as the best solution, allowing local government to build proper, clean and modern homes for the families in inner cities. These souls were the people responsible for the manufacture of all things, thus the growth of the gross domestic product for the country as a whole.

As well as making statutory provision for the building of these houses and rent controls on the existing accommodation, inventive ideas were translated into legislation. Sections 93 to 96 of the 1936 Housing Act - covering 'Housing Associations, & c.' gave opportunity to many after the war to build:

> "**93**.- (1) A Local Authority, for the purpose of this Part of the Act, or a County Council, may promote the formation or extension of, or, subject to the provisions of this Act, assist, a housing association.
> (2) Where a housing association is desirous of erecting houses for the working classes, which in the opinion of the Minister are required, and the Local Authority in the area in which the houses are proposed to be built are unwilling to acquire land with a view

to selling it or leasing it to the association, the county Council, on application of the association, may for this purpose acquire the land and exercise all the powers of a Local Authority under this Part of this Act in regard to the acquisition and disposal of land by local authorities shall apply accordingly."

This legislation enabled a group (a housing association) to be legally constituted for the purpose of building council houses; only if, as stipulated, those houses were to be tenanted by the working population and leased from a local authority or county council. The tenants would subsequently rent these properties from the housing association and the erection of these council houses through self-help would provide additional dwellings for the social housing stock. Further, it allowed an association to acquire land from a local authority through intervention of a county council if necessary. This section of the legislation continued:

"Any such Local Authority or county Council with the consent of, and subject to any regulations or conditions which may be made or imposed by, the Minister, may for the assistance of a housing association-
(a) make grants or loans to the association;
(b) subscribe for any share or loan capital of the association;
(c) guarantee or join in guaranteeing the payment of the principal of and interest on any money borrowed by the association (including any money borrowed as loan capital) or of interest on any share capital issued by the association…"

This part of the legislation enabled, in the vast majority of schemes, financial relief and guarantor support to housing associations.

The Act continues to outline and stipulate that these houses are for those of the working class, and it nominates the specific conditions applied in the Act that would justify the constitution, such as, (Section **94.** – (1) (c):

"provide housing accommodation for persons of the working classes for the purpose of the abatement of overcrowding;"

This was the key statement that would enable those in desperate straits in 1950 to take advantage of this legislation. Further, the Act allowed for the establishment of an umbrella group 'for the purpose of promoting the formation and extension of housing associations and of giving them advice and assistance'. The Act further stipulated that if, five years following the date of the enactment of that legislation, any said 'central association and or body' was in existence, financial assistance for that umbrella group may made available from central government to support its 'activities'. This was to affect one particular group which was very much instrumental in the promotion of the movement for self-help in The Midlands, later in our story.

There is one more piece of evidence that is available to suggest that the government held the notion of self-help very close in its policy to address the housing crisis, but did not quite know how to square the circle. A file exists at the National Archive at Kew from 1945, authored by the Ministry of Works (HLG 101/464) and entitled 'Private Enterprise: Self-Help Schemes', that perfectly illustrates their ideas on how self-help might be pursued and why, at that time, it was not. The main protagonist in the Ministry was a Mr F. J. Root. He called a meeting of various interested members of the Ministry itself and other government departments, on the 10th August 1945 (seven days prior to the end of the Lend-Lease), to examine the possibilities. The bulk of this file is a briefing paper for discussion, with enclosures to be considered. The first page entitled 'Self Help schemes for Housing' poses questions that may be considered and options to discuss, with very pertinent points. Question one concerns the types of self-help housing scheme that might be analysed. Its main focus is the erection of prefabricated houses and removing any obstacles that 'may prevent an individual from building his own house'. He also speculates the possibility of the use of self-help to repair and redecorate existing houses. The catch-all statement at the end of that section is 'any other types of scheme which may be suggested'.

> Question two, which asks:
> "Is it worth examining the possibilities offered by such schemes as a contribution to the housing problem?"

is answered in such a way that there is a suggestion of underlying desperation for all concerned battling with the housing crisis. Mr Root responds to his own question in the following manner:

> "It is suggested that the housing position is such that no possibility should be turned down without examination, unless it is self evidently (sic) absurd."

If we remember, at that time there was still some hope that the temporary housing programme may help to go a long way to remedy the shortfall (it was not until October that those final decisions to curtail that programme were made), it does show that the impending crisis was much worse than previously considered or estimated.

> Question three is a statement to specify the 'advantages offered by self-help schemes', of which there were considered to be two: to 'supplement the types of labour which are scarce', and (b):

> "to provide a psychological outlet by enabling men who cannot obtain houses and wish to do something, to help in providing their own".

It was becoming clear that labour for reconstruction was going to cause an enormous problem; the loss of life and the slow demobilisation of men was just adding to that pressure. The government were facing the realisation that all possible means must be found to extend that workforce as far as possible, and supplement it with others, very probably, unskilled men. The second response to that statement very much became the thrust of the movement that did eventually follow five years later. The enormous sense of achievement that Reg, Harry and Ken felt from being able to 'graft' to produce homes for their families (despite lacking the technical skill) is palpable in each of their interviews; they are incredibly proud of what they had achieved, and quite rightly so.

However, the final statement on the briefing paper, and the conclusion that Mr Root draws, gives a picture of a lack of belief that, without basic prerequisites of building knowledge, only the simplest of construction for houses were going to be possible.
He lists under section 4 entitled 'Some of the difficulties' four key points, the first being the most pertinent and in my opinion why the self-help initiatives were never explored properly at this time:

> "(a) <u>Technical</u> to evolve a structure that can be erected by unskilled or mainly unskilled persons. No one has suggested having an organised scheme for erecting permanent traditional brick houses by self-help methods (skilled individuals might undertake such work, but it would probably not be suitable for an organised scheme).
>
> The suggestions generally are for the erection of prefabricated houses."

It is clear from this that all those who made contributions for this briefing believed emphatically that the building of anything other than a prefabricated house was simply beyond the skills and capacities of anyone outside the trades, and that no ordinary man would even attempt to do so. As such, the schemes that were analysed and then the possible proposals made for the briefing, are limited to that way of thinking. In my opinion, this is one of the main reasons why these limitations did not enable anyone to actually envisage exactly what Mr Root had suggested, '<u>the absurd</u>'.

As they had already ruled out a permanent brick dwelling, the ensuing discussions would revolve around whether this prefabricated structure would be temporary or permanent. With that in mind, he stipulated that there were three further considerations that had to be explored. Firstly, the labour itself. Discussions would have to be made with the industry and careful consideration of the trade unions. Obviously, Mr Root and others envisaged paying professional labour, and issues such as Sunday working and the rates of pay had to be managed carefully. Again, the thought of the average man undertaking these tasks without pay, were not within their remit to consider as an option. The second consideration was how a scheme of this sort was to be financed and whether breakages through lack of skill were going to form part of this budget. More importantly, exactly where these materials were going to be sourced from, and at the time no one envisaged how drastic material shortages were likely to be. The final consideration was that of organisation, and, as far as this group to meet were concerned, that was simple to address by giving direct control and oversight to the Local Authority or the building societies.

Two overseas schemes were analysed and submitted to the group as part of the briefing paper. One was a German emergency housing scheme that existed during the war, and the other a self-help scheme that had been in existence in Stockholm for some time. The German scheme was (as suggested in the title) an emergency solution to an urgent problem. Following the extensive allied bombing of Germany during 1943, a simple two roomed hut that could be erected quickly was made available to those in need in the population. The individuals concerned were issued with a ration book and an instruction booklet, which served as a building licence and enabled them get the necessary prefabricated sections, after they had managed to secure a site to build on from the local authorities. This formal structure would enable the authorities to have oversight and control and support as necessary. The potential householder had to elicit the support of friends and family to help them to build the shelter to the best of their abilities; including the digging and laying of the foundations. The Local Authority would supply the services of electricity and water. These shelters were only 300 sq. ft. in size and consisted of two rooms. There was no bathroom or toilet; the toilet was a separate chemical toilet placed outside.

As basic as these facilities were, this gave Mr Root and his colleagues a point of departure for a potential scheme in the UK. The ration book and the instruction booklet were of interest, as was the concept of the local authority retaining control and oversight. They did speculate that it would be necessary to convince those authorities to make available the necessary materials, while at the same time encouraging the amateur builder to gain as much support as possible from friends and relatives.

The other scheme from Europe that formed part of the briefing paper was from Stockholm. The Ministry of Works had sent a mission there in May of that year to view the project in operation. The extract for those attending the meeting was sub-titled: <u>Municipal Garden Suburb, Stockholm</u>. It opens with commentary regarding the size of plot and house on the original part of the scheme being somewhat smaller, and only containing two-roomed houses. The subsequent houses in the 'small cottage district', are described as containing 'all modern conveniences, gas, hot water, central heating, electric light, W.C. and bathroom and sometimes even a garage'.

The financial requirements of building in the garden suburb, required the 'Stockholmer' (sic) to have accumulated capital of 30%, as mortgages could only be raised against 70% of the taxable value. In comparison, the small cottage scheme only required an investment of a few pounds by the self-builder and ground rent for the first year, as his labour was factored in as 10% of the outlay and the city would then supply 90% of the investment in the form of building materials. The local authority then had control of the planning of the area and the design of the house, and would procure the sub-contractors to supply the necessary electrical, gas and drainage services and foundations, painting etc. There was a brochure available from which the prospective householder could decide on the type of house that they would like to erect.

The pre-requisites were that the potential builder was considered to be 'a good, tax-paying citizen' and their income was not less than £400 per year, and that they had been registered in the city for two years. A detailed questionnaire was then to be answered and submitted, which contained all of this information and questions regarding their present living information (e.g. whether they had a garden or an allotment) and how they intended to conduct the self-build (had they had any previous experience of building and who they were going to get to help them to erect their house-friends and family). Once that had been established, they were issued with a building plot, and the wooden panels and timber were then delivered to that site. From then, the local instructors employed by the municipality would supply the self-builder with technical support and/or training to allow him to commence building and throughout the process until completion. It was noted by the mission that the standardisation of the parts and the organisation of the process led to a very cost-effective outcome, which would be 30% less expensive to the householder had he had it privately built.

3. Desperate times call for...

Three other ideas for schemes were enclosed for the briefing: two with some scant detail and a third not expanded beyond one sentence. The first is proposed by Commander Lambert R. N. (retired). He suggested a scheme that would be situated in rural locations and small towns, and would be centred around those war factory workers and active servicemen that were currently being demobilised from all ranks, enabling them to build within a reasonable distance of their place of work. He suggested that they could be housed in disused barracks and fed by the government and paid via a points system. He had envisaged that, because of the existing military discipline instilled in these men, the process of organised building would be relatively simple; success would be inevitable, as long as some skilled men were available to support the build - at a ratio of one skilled to five unskilled men. He stipulated that materials should be issued free and that the builder should have the right to purchase his property in full via the points system; in his view, this was a just reward for having to build their own home despite returning from a hard, active service. He considered that because of the location of these small business and the time it would take to re-establish products and markets, that it would be beneficial for those companies to be guaranteed a supply of well-located, returning operatives just at the right time, to enable businesses to develop and grow.

The second idea was proposed by Mr T. Fisher, who was a builder of very limited experience, having only built one house pre-war. He had, at the time of supplying information for the briefing paper, just been released from his employment as an inspector in the Ministry of Armaments. He had proposed to employ men part-time, at weekends, to erect prefabs. He had estimated that there could be 3,000 to 5,000 hours of man-power available to do this in the locality of Croydon. He suggested the need to pay these workers on unskilled rates of pay for their time, and that there should be a core of skilled, employed manpower to assist. His personal proposition was to erect a number for 20% less than that of the present costs by installation contractors. The final submission for the briefing was a suggestion that the Home Guard and Fire Guard had been asked for suggestions: no such submissions had been included.

In my opinion, it was in part due to the haste in which these submissions were called for, combined with the lack of experience and practice of these methods within the UK, that there was very little substance contained in the UK-led ideas that had been proposed, as compared to those much more expansive concepts from Germany and Sweden. The documentation that followed from the meeting called on the 10th August 1945 is interesting to read. In the opening statement a note has been made that even if there were never a large number of houses built through self-help methods, the psychological benefits to those building would be of great value, and that those people must feel encouraged in their efforts by those in authority.

The enclosure that follow contain proposed types of house that may be built under a self-build scheme, again with a statement that, as these buildings had to be simple to erect, traditional brick construction had to be ruled out. As such, only a timber prefabricated construction, or one built using Invicta building blocks, would be considered suitable. It was added that a lightweight, steel-frame prefab may be possible with some technical support. The financial and organisational aspects were thought to be out of the reach of most who may consider building; as such, it was the opinion of the panel that a Local Authority should assume control. As to how finances were to be raised and materials procured, those aspects still needed further research.

The conclusions of the meeting were that the idea should be pursued, and that two technical panels should convene at the Ministry to explore the concepts in greater detail, such as the design and build, and the procurement of materials and finances. It was envisaged that these schemes might have commenced in the spring of 1946 and that POW's might be used to make the necessary site preparations. The very final point in this document is most telling, especially when you consider the date that these notes were compiled (18th August, 1945; the Lend-Lease had ceased the day before). The note reads:

> "The Controller of Building Materials, Ministry of Works, should be asked to consider whether in the light of the new war situation, it was still considered that supply considerations ruled out the possibility of a simple prefabricated timber house being supplied for the scheme."

A technical panel must have met within days, as a week after these notes were drafted a further paper was issued to clarify the conclusions drawn by those who met. Within those notes it is clear that any timber house was completely abandoned due to shortage of the supply of timber. The Ministry had gone as far as preparing sketches for a modest bungalow using Invicta building blocks, but stressed a large proportion of skilled man-hours would still be required for the erection of these houses: foundations, drains, electrical services, chimney erection and roof tiling. Following, it was proposed that the Uni-seco prefab may be the way forward for those with limited skill to build, but the questions of financial support and eventual ownership still remained unanswered.

Two more memoranda are enclosed on the file. Their authorship is not possible to determine, but it is probable to assume they came from the Ministry of Health under the leadership of Nye Bevan, who of course was the Minister for Housing. The first memo confirms much of what has already been articulated in the previous papers. The final memo states the following:

> "11th October, 1945
>
> Dear Root,
>
> <u>Self-Help Schemes for Housing</u>
>
> At the meeting of 7th September it was agreed that we should let you know whether we thought that this scheme should be proceeded with. We agree, of course, with you that all possible help and encouragement should be given to people who are so enterprising as to wish to build their houses with their own hands but in view of the byelaw and planning position and the fact that we are not prepared to agree to a Uni-seco type of house as a permanent house, as stated in your paper of the 23rd August, a timber house is ruled out by the supply position, we have come to the conclusion, that it is not worth while going on with the scheme.
>
> The Department of Health for Scotland have been consulted and are of the same opinion."

3. Desperate times call for…

      With the acute shortages that the country was now being faced with, and an emergency housing programme for half a million homes that was only going to deliver one third of that number, it seems that proposals to allow men to build their own homes using these methods were not feasible. Nye Bevan had been most vociferous in his pronouncements that housing should be given to those in greatest need in the first instance; that would mean those in the most severe areas of deprivation. As materials and manpower were in such short supply, this necessitated the rationing of everything, including building licences. The council house programme was the only direction that the government could take. Consequently, a possible scheme designed for those with enterprise to build for themselves remained on the shelves in Whitehall. It was still a good idea, just not at the right time, and without the large amount of support that government believed would be required, it was simply not feasible. That was until desperation from all quarters drove those of the same mind to consider what may have been quite an 'absurd' idea as a possible (and most practical solution) to aid the housing crisis.

Chapter 4

Fifty men of Brum

It is an interesting moment for an author, when you are two-thirds of your way through writing a book, having compiled many hours (in some cases many months and years) of painstaking research. You think that you know the story and that those few scant bits of information that you have so far failed to uncover cannot be of any great significance. Otherwise, there would be more than a trace of any record remaining, and those 'happenings' would have had greater significance, thus, have remained in the 'folklore' memory.

When I set to writing this book a few months ago, I was at that point. I had spent two years researching, and becoming familiar with my research. I had put a puzzle together in my mind, and found a chronological order by which to narrate it all to enable an ease of understanding to you, the reader. So, I set to write. Meanwhile, one incident and one character that, in my opinion, has particular significance to all that happened, continued to evade me. Despite constant searching, either through interviews with those that are left, or searches through local and national archives, only very scant traces remained. That is, until I sat at my computer 24 hours ago, having finally correctly identified the name of a road (indistinctly heard in one of the audio playbacks from the interviews), and having entered that name into my computer search bar, with the addition of the words 'self-build'. Up it popped, the evidence that connects all and provides that essential missing piece of the puzzle; the piece that had fallen down the back of the sofa, so to speak.

In all the three interviews; with Reg, Harry and Ken, and in the Solihull UDC minutes, National Archives at Kew, and even the speech given by Martin Lindsay MP, there is a reference to another scheme, that of the Post Office Workers of Sheldon and the name of one particular individual: Mr George Lavender. The piece of evidence that I have now uncovered, thankfully, is a brief but insightful cameo into that particular scheme and some explanation of George Lavender, whose name will keep reappearing throughout part 2 of this book (the main story of our scheme and its place within the Solihull UDC narrative). I hope my interpretation in all that now follows goes some way to rehabilitating Mr Lavender, who I believe may have become a victim of the self-interest of another, much larger, organisation. In my opinion, George had good intentions from the outset, and did all that he had to do, until it became obvious that to make that advice pay served two purposes: one, it enabled him to devote more time to the scheme that he had instigated, and two, there was an opening for an advisor to the local self-help movement that was rapidly emerging. He realised that there was an opportunity for someone with his knowledge, and he took it. Sometimes there is no harm in showing a bit of initiative; it seems this was his trademark.

I make no apologies for naming this chapter after one of the sources that I will now share for this story (my lucky find). It is an extremely apt title and an excellent description of the 'matter-of-fact' approach that was taken by them all. In my speculative search of the internet, I came across both articles on the same Labour Party website: 'Think Left'. The first article was "Fifty Men of Brum" authored by Willi Frischaur, dated October 8th 1949, featured in *Illustrated*, and the second was its corresponding sequel article (author unknown), entitled "Build-our-own-home families move in" dated December 1951 and featured in the *John Bull* magazine. In the 1951 article there is a link to *Pathe News* that I must share with you, and I implore anyone who is interested to go to this link on the internet and watch the short film, as it is worth a thousand words and helps to set the drama of this complete story to the greatest effect. The film is entitled 'Legion Builders (1949) can be found on YouTube: https://youtu.be/ASGDqMP9FdE

It all began for this group and this particular man in the way it did for so many: the return of a soldier – following his stint in active service for his country – to a war-shattered economy, and a bomb-damaged city. George Lavender was one such man. He had spent his war as a paratrooper (Airborne Signals) reaching the rank of sergeant. This was to stand him in good stead as a leader of men. He was set apart by his age as well as his rank, for when George returned from the Middle East in 1946 to marry his girl, he was 48 years old. Whether he returned to a position that had been held open, or was recruited for his skills in the aftermath, still remains a mystery. We find George in 1947 as a post office engineer based at the Fordrough Lane depot in Birmingham. He is also at that time (probably through his rank and age) the assistant secretary of the British Legion that meets there. This group, for any younger members reading this book, was the for ex-servicemen, and had a very strong membership nationally, having had two grand conflagrations in just over a period of two decades: many men clung to their comradeship in peace time that had been so dominant in their lives for so long

It was through the various meetings of this particular group in Fordrough Lane, where the common moans and groans of the time were often heard. The statistics given in the 1949 article support much of what I have already recorded: by October 1949, the government had only achieved the building of 541,531 permanent homes, and, according to the article, there were still '157,146' families living under temporary roofs. The city, having suffered more than most, had responded with haste:

> "Birmingham was building fast-by now 3,395 permanent and 4,625 temporary houses had been put up by the Local Authority and 1,665 by private concerns but not swift enough for fifty ex-servicemen."

Indeed, with a waiting list of 70,000 in 1947, not fast enough for many in the city, as we shall find. However, this particular group met regularly, though some not often as they should, which prompted George Lavender to ask the question why not. According the second article, the invariable response was; 'We'd like to come but we can't leave the wife alone in rooms. It would be different if we had a house.' Whether it was Bill Spencer, the chairman of that branch of the British Legion, who incited movement with his statement 'Let's build some houses then', or George Lavender with the response: 'Why not build our own homes? The best way to get things done is to roll up your sleeves and start to work', the idea to do it themselves took hold. It was certainly George who got things moving and then continued to oversee all operations for the duration of that particular scheme. Many of the men expressed enthusiasm, and wanted to join. After all, this was the only opportunity that they could see for having the house that they and their wives dreamed of. George had married Eileen Hart the previous year and she was expecting their first child (Barry), but as a couple they had absolutely no chance of advancing up that very long list of names.

Together, George and Bill took to their bicycles. They knew that the first problem to address was land (as I have stressed, so much was either bomb-damaged, or had been ear-marked by Birmingham Corporation for their council house building). The only thing to do was cycle around the city, seeking out any tracts of available land. On one of these sorties from the city, George and Bill arrived in the Sheldon area (half of Sheldon fell under the auspices of Solihull UDC and the other half under Birmingham Corporation). They were near what was then George V Memorial Park (known at that time as National Trust property and never to be developed), this is the site where Sheldon Manor (West Manor) used to stand and is now called Sheldon Country Park. They may well have found undeveloped roads that had been laid out during the interwar years around that area (there were many around Sheldon in both Local Authority districts). They were able to ascertain that the land was privately owned, and that there were many plots available from the land-owner with a 99-year lease.

We have to remember that much of what George and Bill were doing at this time was ground-breaking work; no one had ever attempted this, they had absolutely no idea how to proceed. Most of what followed was down to lucky advice, happenstance and a great deal of detective work. George had a friend who was an architect in Birmingham and he sought his advice. Lockersley Hare told George that he was aware of the Swedish schemes for self-help, and asked George what sort of bungalow he wished to build. This speed of reaction had rather over-taken the man from the British Legion who had not considered the idea that far, however, he knew that first he must consult with the others of the scheme and, in particular, the wives. However, this was assuming that the scheme had licences to build in the first place (at that time George and Bill had not made that enquiry) but, George (ever the optimist) assured Lockersley he had licences. Lockersley was invited to a meeting of the collective and their wives and as George recalls:

"He just drew a rectangle on the board… and the womenfolk filled it in."

The bungalow as was planned, would comprise of: three bedrooms, a living room, a kitchen, a bathroom and a separate WC. It would have a good-sized garden and a space for a garage to be erected at some future date.

Both Bill Spencer and George Lavender knew that there would be a certain amount of red-tape involved; everything at that time required some sort of permit, or licence, or there were umpteen Ministry circulars constantly being updated with new standing instructions from the Ministry of Housing. The best thing that both men could do was to seek legal opinion as to how they should proceed and what their next moves should be. They managed to discuss their ideas with conveyancing solicitor, who suggested that they needed to seek the advice of a barrister. At first, the barrister in question was somewhat confused by their intentions: how any man without skill could even consider a scheme of this complexity or scale was beyond him, however, after a fortnight of deliberation and consultation of the various housing acts, he met with the two men at his chambers in the city. He advised them that if they formed as;

"…an association under a Trust Deed, thus avoiding stamp duties and Schedule "A" income tax payable if they registered under the Companies Act…"

That further they could:

"…arrange mortgages, lease land and get permission to build."

Additionally, as they would be an association that rented the houses to their members, each house could qualify for a government subsidy of £16/10 per year, payable for 60 years, and that as renting tenants, they could apply for licences from the Local Authority's allocation of council house licences (that as we know at that time was a ratio of four council house licences to one private build licence). Thus, was born the Post Office Branch, British Legion Housing Association.

At that point, George had forty-nine committed members, all ex-servicemen, many of them Post Office engineers, or Post Office mechanics, but only one with actual building experience - Fred Moss, a builder's foreman. How George then managed to secure the twenty-four licences to build the first twelve pairs, whether they were issued with the first 10, next 10 and so on, is unclear. While the negotiations were on-going with Birmingham Council for the licences, finance had to be raised, and obviously, the men had to learn to build.

The initial capital was raised by securing £20 from each of the members; not an easy undertaking for any of them, George then made approaches to various building societies with the idea and the architect's plans. All but one either failed to respond or knocked back the idea, however, one society was inspired by the concept to suggest an astonishing £1,000 per house (they estimated each would cost £600 to build). This mortgage was offered over a thirty-year term, interest payable at an annual rate of four percent. George states in the article that the association opted for the thirty-year term, as most were thirty years old and they would all be looking to retire by the time the mortgage was repaid (George was fifty by now; there was never going to be the opportunity for him to repay his mortgage). The mortgage was a 'progressive one' payable in four-stage payments: damp-proof course level (DPC), plate height, topping off (roof), and all fittings in. All stages of the build would need to be regularly inspected, to release funds at each stage.

With the security of having raised the mortgage for the members and possessing the initial capital and land, but still awaiting licences, George set about ordering the needed equipment and initial materials. They had a site, they had time while they waited on the licences, and this would be the best opportunity to train the men in the various skills that they would need to build a house. It is important to point out here that this lack of skill (and the large number of men involved) is probably why the Post Office workers finished a long time after my parents' scheme, which started much later. The Post Office workers were always going to be slow in their progress. The skills needed to be a bricklayer, a plasterer or a carpenter are not picked up in a few training sessions on a building site; most qualified individuals had undertaken a skilled apprenticeship of seven years' duration. This group of men did not have seven years, but they did have determination, and they did have George Lavender's leadership skills.

The father of one of the members was a Clerk of Works - Mr W. A. Olsson. The group managed to find a church hall with a piece of land adjacent where they could meet twice a week and, under the direction of Mr Olsson, learned to be bricklayers. Meanwhile, each member continued to pay a subscription of 3s 6d per week. This enabled all of the administration to be carried out and the various other extraneous costs to be met. George had managed to purchase three Nissan huts that would be excellent for storing all of the needed material as they were purchased and it would also provide that space for meetings on-site as required. He also acquired a lorry, very probably from the same source as our scheme did, which I believe was the Post Office Fordrough Lane Depot.

From May till October 1949:

"...began a training period of more than six months during which the men spent the leisure hours - every evening and every weekend - building walls and pulling them down, mixing concrete, handling trowels..."

During that time, they did achieve their licences, or at least the first few. George had made a 'gentleman's agreement' with the landlord for the remaining 13 plots of land that would be required when the final 26 licences became available. It has to be remembered that this scheme was comprised of active servicemen in their early thirties; they were used to taking orders and used to the necessity of discipline. Collectively, they managed to design an exacting points system for allocation, which would enable those with greatest need to have the first houses available, but retain a competitive edge, as any time wasted or not committed to could amount to a deduction of points, thus, move that member down the housing priority list. As such, you were highest priority based on the length of your marriage and the number of children that you had. The list was so drawn that each of the members' names had five squares spaced between them. For every half-an-hour a member failed to work, a square would be marked. If a member lost a full hour, they were moved down a place on the priority list.

From the outset, the group made the collective decision as to what their overall time commitment should be to the scheme. Again, these men had no idea how long it would take them to complete one pair of bungalows, never mind the first 12 pairs, and they would still have 26 members waiting to build for after that first allocation of 24 licences had been erected. Each member was required to work three evenings a week for three hours, from 6.15pm to 9.15pm, and this was on top of their normal full-time employment for the Post Office. They were also required to work each Saturday and Sunday on their self-build scheme. They were only to allow themselves one day for a holiday a year and that was to be Christmas Day. They knew that, whatever the weather, in daylight or at night under floodlight, they must maintain their tempo in order for all of their forty-nine other comrades to gain a home for their family as quickly as physically possible.

Sometime in the summer of 1949, the Post Office Workers of Fordrough Lane obtained permission to build from the local Council and the regional board for the Ministry of Health. The training classes that they had undertaken, and their innate skills as engineers and mechanics, combined to produce reasonably competent builders, if a little slow. They had managed, by the date of the first article in early October 1949, to have their first bungalow near to completion and were celebrating that fact. Tommy Morris, who was thirty-one with two children, was to be the first member of the scheme to take up occupation. According to their priority list that was in evidence, their scheme would allocate the second to Mr and Mrs Lewis with their daughter; the third to William Spencer with his wife and child; then Jack Ward with his wife and daughter; the fifth would be Eric Meigh with his wife and child; and the sixth would be Bert Jones with his wife and child (that was assuming at the time that those six members would continue with their same commitment and determination and not slip back on the priority list). There is a note in that first article regarding the reaction that the scheme initially received from the trades unions within the building trades. It is to the effect that, as they were considered to be relieving some of the pressure of work from some of the union members in the building trade, that they were generally accepted. The inference being that there had been times during that very early stage that they did experience a certain amount of antagonism (maybe even hostility) from other union members, who may have perceived the amateurs as taking away their livelihoods.

We move now to reflecting mainly on the article published two years later in December 1951, in the *John Bull* magazine. Much can be viewed as hindsight consideration of their 1949 experience, although in 1951 the scheme is still very much a work-in-progress. They have in that two-year period managed to house twenty-one of the fifty members. They are still not half way through and they have endured a few interesting twists and turns along the way. However, they have also received considerable national recognition and attention, which George Lavender has by now translated into a professional career and personal commitment; one that would have eventual consequences for his personal and professional life.

Obviously, the printing of the first article back in 1949 prompted a considerable amount of local and national attention. Locally, it stimulated many, like the hero of this book, Reg Harvey, to seek George Lavender out, to find out how to make it happen. I feel that it is important to place George Lavender within his context as he seems to have been much maligned by some, yet, there appears no actual evidence to suggest inappropriate or illegal undertakings of any nature. Who was George Lavender? And what impression would one have grasped upon meeting him – particularly if you were a young ex-serviceman too?

It is obvious that George had something about him, an air of authority. Within the second article, the correspondent refers to him as 'a jovial hustler' with his 'strong jaw' and 'receding hairline'. George Lavender was 53 by then, not a young man. He had seen active service as a senior NCO and he would have been of an age to have been a sergeant to my father early on in the war had they been in the same regiment. There is no doubt that he earned that right to be sergeant, and having viewed the *Pathe News* film, he does appear to be an 'alpha' figure, displaying both the presence and body language. I would also speculate that, as those from other schemes sought him out for advice and direction, so his own scheme (which consisted mainly of men 20 years younger than himself - but by no means young naïve men; very much war-hardened and experienced) looked up to him for leadership, structure and guidance.

The scheme is referred to as his idea, in various parts of the articles. In fact, in the second article, the news reporter notes that the others in the scheme refer to George as 'the great white chief'; they would have deferred to him, both in age and rank, but I would argue that, had he misled or conned them, he would not have lasted a month leading that scheme (never-mind the three and half years that it did actually take). If he had either been inept, incompetent, or even, as some may infer, a crook, they would have ousted him. These men were all the same age as my father, and Harry Pestridge; they were neither young nor green, and they were all mechanics or engineers.

As I have eluded to, George was sought out by many people; even the camera crews came to record this amazing happening in Sheldon, Birmingham. Its seems that it was not just those other prospective self-helpers that took interest, but also the land agents Shipway and Doble (John Doble was responsible for making regular inspections to ensure all was up to scratch). He became impressed with George and his ability to network and get up and actually do something. It is recorded in this second article that, by that stage, George had given up his full-time job at the Post Office Depot in Fordrough Lane, and become the man to facilitate the self-help schemes around The Midlands. In fact, Shipway and Doble had given him an office and a Dictaphone and let him work out of their agency. A mutually-beneficial partnership was in operation, he could help to identify the forming groups and direct them towards Shipway and Doble, and they in turn could find them plots of land to lease.

I know from other sources that this self-styled, self-help, umbrella association became known as the 'Central Association for Self-Help', and George Lavender was it. Of course, giving up the day job had consequences; he had to earn a salary somehow, and it is noted in this article that he was taking a commission for various services. This would eventually be used against him. However, the National Federation of Housing Associations that would in 1952 take overall control, would demand subscriptions from their members; would sell their advice through pamphlets and journals; and would be in a receipt of a grant from the government under the 1936 Housing Act as the representative umbrella group. So, whatever the false perceptions of George Lavender that were created and facilitated at the time to disenfranchise him, it did not mean that he was doing anything that would not be done by another, much bigger, organisation one year later and be considered absolutely legal.

By the heady times of the 1951 article, all was 'on the up' for George Lavender: he and his wife had moved into their bungalow with their four-year-old son Barry, and twenty other families were now in occupation in their homes. The bungalows were now being valued at £2000 (each having cost below £1000 to build) and having achieved a mortgage of £1000 towards the material for each one.

As one might expect, there had been a few incidents of difficultly, such as inspections that had failed to pass muster with the local surveyor, causing the odd tile to be replaced. Even a member being a little too creative with the glazing bars on a window, contrary to the architect's plans, literally had to be changed at the very last minute when an inspection had been due. There were odd mishaps too: one man falling into a concrete-filled trench; another - an electrician as reported in the article - falling through a ceiling as the plasterers were admiring their finished work. This did cause some to 'cuss', but there were plenty of laughs and a great deal of 'comradeship'. The wives were regular visitors and came to make tea and refreshments, and a fish and chip van called to site daily.

There had only been one major hiccup: that of the remaining thirteen plots of land. When George went to redeem the pledge of the 'gentleman's handshake', he found that Birmingham City Council had made a 'compulsory purchase' of that land. This left George no other alternative but to approach Birmingham Housing Committee himself to appeal for the land for the members of the association.

As it happens, this compulsory purchase had coincided with the back-lash that was beginning against council houses: with so many sites having been developed in such a short time across the city, this was going to work in the scheme's favour. When local residents had heard of the compulsory purchase order on this land, and gained the further knowledge that the Council intended to develop more Corporation houses, the residents had objected strongly. Faced with a local rebellion, and the 'lot of the poor self-helpers' who were very much in the public-eye, combined with the persuasive presence of George Lavender, the chairman of the committee suggested that the locals may object less if it were allocated to the self-build scheme. This did cause a significant delay of four and half months to their build

4. Fifty men of Brum

whilst they waited for approval. In December 1951, the scheme members were projecting a work-timeline of another eighteen months before they would all be housed; I would like to assume that this was the case and I can uncover no evidence either way.

Both articles do give the impression of considerable camaraderie, of learning by mistakes (and they did have a few of those) that is to be expected from infant-builders that had acquired the necessary skills as they went along. Some might accuse them of being 'hobbyist'; I do not think so. Just because construction was not their trade (they were engineers and mechanics by occupations), they were all hard-working men, and all had backgrounds in manual trades; they turned their hands to most things. There is no evidence of any external sub-contracting for any part of their scheme; all was done in-house so to speak, by the members of the scheme. I do feel that their lack of practice and technique would have slowed them down considerably and it may well have led to financial over-stretching towards the end of their scheme, as the money available via the mortgage to build was less than the actual build costs involved by that stage. However, whatever these men lacked in skill they more than made up for in sheer determination. They all ended up with a house on a nominal rent of thirty shillings and sixpence a week. The last words in this chapter should go to George, as he was one of the first that Reg Harvey sought advice from. Towards the end of the 1951 article George states that:

> "All sorts of people come to me," he says, "some in overalls, others with briefcases. They all ask if there is a vacancy in one of my groups, I tell them that there isn't, but if they are the right type, they'll form a group of their own. Then I can help them."

Part 2

'There hangs a tale'

Chapter 5

From little acorns…

To me as a researcher and writer, this is where the story becomes particularly interesting. My project has always been to save 'the voice'; to conserve the living history before it leaves us through death. Strangely, the story that my brother and I know least about, is that of our own parents. Yes, we were always told things, as parents recount their lives from time to time to their children, but as is the way of the young we probably listened with half an ear. As a consequence, the story we tell of their lives is second-hand (as they are both long since gone), a jigsaw of fragments that we have cross-checked through the accounts of others, and that is no longer verifiable with our own parents. As the author, it would be my first thought to start with their story in this part of the book, but as a researcher, valuing and meriting those living voices, I shall place my parents' story somewhere towards the middle of this opening. This is a chapter of introductions: to the main protagonists of the scheme, to the concept itself and to those still left to tell the tale.

Reg Harvey was born in 1927. For the first four years of his life he lived in a Birmingham telephone exchange, where his mother ran daytime operations and had oversight of the girls that worked there, and his father was the night operator. As these exchanges became automated, so the operators such as Reg's parents became surplus to requirements and had to seek housing elsewhere. It was at this point in 1931 that Reg moved to a Council estate in Weoley Castle in Birmingham. It was also where Reg made numerous friends who all liked to play 'games' as he puts it; boy's games, but not the sort of games that would get you in to too much trouble:

"I mean you didn't in those days, did you?" He remarks dryly.

He tells a story of being up a tree nearby to home, and a bobby on his bicycle just passing by at the wrong time, with the familiar click, click of the bicycle and spotting the young offender upon the tree:

"Come down laddie." Came the stern voice.

Reg duly obeyed, but once he was within reach of the policeman, his backside was smacked throughout his unceremonious descent. A further reprimand was given, that of informing his father the next time: that put the 'fear of God' into Reg. That was the era when young people respected their elders and especially their parents, and policemen were to be obeyed at all times: suffice to say he never risked the same endeavour again. Council estates were places that were aspired to, where all wanted to live; the idea of the garden town or village with green spaces, inside lavatories and bathrooms, and warm coal fires, was a complete contrast to the slums that were still to be cleared.

The education that Reg received was somewhat disjointed. He had attended grammar school briefly, but, being a non-fee-paying boy, had experienced bullying: having his hand-stitched badge, which marked him out as from the lower class, ripped from his

5. From little acorns…

blazer on several occasions. Eventually his father had to buy him out for the princely sum of £5. Added to this, it was a time of air raids and evacuations, which caused further disruption to his education; he was briefly evacuated to Gloucestershire and returned quickly. All these interruptions meant that at the age of 14 in 1941, he became a boy messenger in the G.P.O., and upon passing his exams, a telegraphist. The most significant moment for Reg during his early career in the G.P.O. was when the captivating and beautiful Dot caught his eye; she was a telegraphist too, and her looks were striking:

"Very like the Hollywood actress Dorothy Lamour", he muses.

Dot had a very different start in life to Reg, having originally lived in Northfield, (then in Worcester, now Birmingham) in a council house. Her mother wanted a larger house, and it just so happened that one became available through the Bournville Village trust in Selly Oak; a beautiful village, originally designed to house the workers from Cadbury's. She reminisces that sometime later, her father had an option to purchase the house, but he refused on the grounds that he believed that home-ownership was a 'millstone around your neck'. When Birmingham Corporation bought up the properties, they became tenants to that Council.

Their house was opposite Cadbury's Manor Farm. The farmer, being the enterprising sort, gave five equal shares in a pig for coupons and household waste for the swill. Every day, the five households with a share would deposit their waste in a dustbin, which the farmer would collect to fatten the pig; from that came an ample supply of bacon, chops and ham: quite a treat for those suffering the effects of wartime rationing. Occasionally, her father would 'flush out' for the farmer and bring home a brace of pigeons or rabbits.

Dot went to an ordinary school, not unusual for girls at that time, who were assumed to marry and become housewives eventually. She is highly intelligent and could read avidly before anyone realised in her family, until one day at the very tender age of 5, she read out the headline on the 'News of the World' newspaper, to the shock and horror of her mother, who made sure the paper was not purchased again. She entered the General Post Office (G.P.O.) and passed her exams quickly to become a telegraphist. Reg had always admired Dot from afar with her long black hair. He lived at the back of her house, as he says, 'in the common council houses' and he often saw her walking down the hill. Reg was always the very determined sort: he describes himself as devious even then. He made up his mind that she was the girl for him, he just had to figure out a strategy to woo and win her, so he set his mind to a plan. He had noted the bus that she took each day to work, and he would wait and watch and make sure that he got the same bus but two stops later. He was noticed but, as this was the time for shy, demure, young ladies, ignored.

Dot probably had it in her mind that he was the young man who was regularly 'mentioned in dispatches'; notes were often passed at work, to the effect that there was a young gentleman that admired her. Again, Dot rebuffed this. The moments that finally sealed their relationship were actually due to the war and blackouts. It was a time when young women were to be protected by young men in society, and the G.P.O. had issued all men with a lamp to accompany those young ladies working late home in the blackout. One night, the request came to anyone who lived near Dot to escort her and Reg was there. They have been married for 70 years: quite a determined achievement.

Reg was called up in 1945 while they were courting. He had spent 18 months working in the Civilian Technical Corps in Kidderminster; the forces had taken over a radio

5. From little acorns...

station prior to the second front opening. There was just too great a volume of communications traffic for the enlisted services to handle, hence the need for volunteer communications technicians, and this stood him in good stead for his army service. Unfortunately for Reg, his call up coincided with the final months of the war. As he says, he was due to go into the army and then the Japanese surrendered. Had his call-up not happened for a few months more, he would have just had to endure two years of National Service; unfortunately, as he was already in, he had three years to do; he wrote to Dot every day and each day she wrote back.

He was posted to Germany. It was the time of non-fraternisation and Belsen, however, he reflects that he did have 'one or two good jobs there'. Having two trades, both as a telegraphist and a wireless operator, he was a lead reserve. One assignment put him as the regular escort to the King's Messenger, crossing into Berlin with the diplomatic bag and a grumpy diplomat. Reg and Dot married while he was still on service in 1947. From that day, Reg moved into his in-laws' house in Selly Oak; they had one room to sleep in and one room as a parlour. By the time Reg was demobbed, he was sharing a house with Dot, her mother and father, and her elder sister Irene, who had two children. As the house was so overcrowded, Irene had to live apart from her husband (who was Reg's brother), and that gave the couple a higher priority for a council house. Reg knew at that time that Dot and himself were way down the list, at approximately 68,900.

At this point, I will turn to the next key figure in the scheme, Mr Harry Pestridge and his wife Joan. Harry was born and lived in Selly Park in Birmingham, on the banks of the river Rea. He was the oldest member of the scheme and at the time of the interview with my brother was about to turn 100 years old (sadly he died while the research was being conducted for this book). His father was an upholsterer, as were his five brothers. His mother and sister were French polishers; a family of 9. Harry undertook a seven-year apprenticeship as a bricklayer, near Wolverhampton. He started at 14 and, because of the depression, they were always on the road. Joan was from the centre of the city, having lived in the area called Duddeston. She was born in Loveday Street Hospital (as my father had been in 1917 and myself in 1963); she was christened in St Anne's church in Duddeston. Her father had been an electrician and then served as a regular in the navy; after the Dardanelles, he was let go and, with it being 'hard times', found it difficult to get employment. Joan had a basic education and, with the war breaking out, she left at 13 and went to work for a saddle-makers in Livery Street. It is there (through one of his sisters-in-law) that she met Harry sometime later.

Harry, meanwhile, was called up and although he hardly mentions his war service, according to Ken Quiney and Reg Harvey, he was a senior NCO. He spent some time guarding the Suez Canal, where his excellent construction skills meant he was able to build decoy targets to fool the German bombers and protect the canal. He managed to erect a sizeable scaffold rigged with lights, which they would move around; one Italian bomber even crashed because the decoy was so effective. Back in civilian life, Harry became a clerk of works for various contractors. There was a considerable amount of building work to be done in the Birmingham area, and the two main chains of public houses at that time (Ansells and M and B breweries) needed pubs repairing and, in some cases, building. Harry and Joan married in 1949, at St Mathews Church, in Great Francis Street. Initially they lived with Harry's parents, but as one might imagine, with such a large family (although many had

5. From little acorns...

married and moved on), that was quite complicated. After a while, they moved in with Joan's mother in Duddeston Mill Road (her father had died). Their daughter was born there in 1950.

The next brief cameo is that of Ken Quiney and his late wife Pauline. Ken was born in Montgomery Street, Sparkbrook, Birmingham. Despite being an only child until he was nine (when two sisters eventually arrived) his parents found that life was hard. As he says, there was no family allowance then and there was only two years in age between the daughters. They could ill-afford for him to attend grammar school; he did but, being the only one from his area, he had a particularly rough time. Ken describes it as a 'dog's life' and he really did not want to go. Eventually, he sat his exams for the G.P.O., passed, and was taken in as a boy messenger. Following a short while in that role, he passed the further exams and became a telegraphist.

In 1943, he was called up to a very specialised unit - The Air Formation Signals. It was a combination of the army and the RAF: very self-contained, with only 40 men (half were trained telephonists and operators, the other half were linesmen and engineers). Whenever the army commandeered an airfield in France, or Germany, this unit was sent in to set up the communications and 'man' the communications traffic on a 24 watch. He was in Germany when the war ended but, unfortunately, it meant that his role had stopped, so as he was under 25 and single he was brought back to the UK, where they were regrouped. Luckily for Ken, he was on embarkation leave ready to be shipped to the Far East when Japan announced its surrender. All was not over, as it was decided that these men should now go to Egypt, just as Palestine destabilised. The consequence of this was a posting there. As Ken says, they were getting shot at by everyone - Arabs and Jews alike - and they were pulled back to Egypt and the Suez: it was from there he was finally demobbed. He left Egypt on the SS Staffordshire bound for Liverpool to be released at York in an oversized suit with a trilby hat. Like many who were called up, his clothes had been sent home, and a combination of a developing young man being fed a good diet, he found that nothing fitted him once he was back home.

He went back to the G.P.O. Many of the women found the demobilised servicemen to be a problem: as more of these men returned back to their positions, there was less need for their female colleagues' services. However, Ken was then sent for his exams to enter the Civil Service and, having passed those, he was posted to the National Assistance Board and based in Walsall. He feels that this was quite timely for his parents, as they had been bombed-out in Sparkbrook and it was good fortune for Ken to have a friend that he could stay with in Rushall. One of the women who had been particularly vocal about the return of servicemen posing a problem for the women employed at the G.P.O. was Pauline, who would later become his wife. He speaks wistfully of how he had always admired her. It was during one of her particularly vocal exchanges that Ken plucked up the courage to ask what she would do if he asked her out on a date. Her reply was quick and to the point, as one might expect from Pauline:

"What took you so long?"

As I have briefly explained, my father Joseph Debney and mother came from very different backgrounds as individuals, and this was a true tale of wartime romance throwing unlikely people together through circumstance. My father was in the Royal Artillery throughout his war service, and generally took all of his leave back at his parent's house in Ward End in Birmingham. However, on this particular occasion, either because he was

5. From little acorns...

billeted nearby or because he was in transit, he was in Leicester in 1940 during the height of the Blitz, which was probably April of that year. My mother, Margaret Flynn, seemed to have spent her whole life in transit. At that time, she was 20 years old and in such a short time span had been through much and many miles of travel.

She had been born on a Saskatchewan prairie in 1919 in a particularly heavy winter where they were snowed in for six months. Her parents, both from Glasgow, were of Irish descent. By the time she was three and half, she had lost her father through heart failure, her mother to peritonitis, and her brother had been kicked to death by a wild horse. She and her surviving sister were shipped to Scotland to her elderly grandparents in Dunoon. Unfortunately, by the age of 17 she was once again an orphan, and having suffered a convent education followed by commercial college in Glasgow, she set out for London to work as a secretary. During this time, she was lucky to apply for - and had been accepted by - the Slade College of Art (she was a fine water-colourist), but war was on the horizon and all opportunities in that direction ceased.

Life took on a whole new meaning for my mother once the phoney war of the first year subsided: she had found herself evacuated to a hostel in Leicester. She often described the story to me of the nights that the parachute mines fell on Victoria Park, and one night in particular when she was descending the stairs in the hostel. She heard - the by now – the familiar swish, swish, that propelled everyone into mortal fear. At the time, she had been rushing to take shelter, only a little too late, and the landing window blew in on her, badly cutting her face and embedding bits of glass in her skin. She made her way to the nearest first aid point, and noticed that all the silver birch trees in the park now looked like ghosts in the moonlight, as they had been stripped of their bark. At the first aid point she was duly bandaged up and dispatched to the nearest shelter: it was there she first caught sight of my father. As she used to say, he was cowering in the corner with a healthy tan, as she entered battered and bruised from all the action; it seemed strange that the civilian suffered, while the serviceman did not. There started a wartime courtship, including the other anecdote of my father taking her out on a date in Birmingham later that year in November to celebrate her 21st birthday; the night that the Luftwaffe smashed Coventry. They could see the glow of all the fires in the skies, but were turned back by an ARP warden exclaiming:

"Coventry's had it."

By February 1941, they were married in Birmingham, and for a while my mother lived in cramped conditions with her in-laws, sharing a bed with my father's 15-year-old sister. They managed to find a flat in Handsworth, in Park Avenue, in the same house as another who I shall recount the story of - Beryl Rose. It was through this connection that my parents would be introduced to the scheme. My mother had my elder sister Diana Patricia in 1943; unfortunately, she failed to thrive and died the following year. In 1945, my parents managed to find their flat in Bromford Lane and my mother lived there alone until my father was demobbed in 1946. After a brief stint back at the Co-operative, he was employed as a finance officer at Highcroft Hall Mental Hospital. By the end of 1948, my mother was expecting my brother James, who was born the following May.

Mrs Pat Rowson was born in Kings Norton. She was fortunate in her education, attending the Bournville Non-Denominational School, which had an endowment from Cadbury. During the war, when she was 12, she became a volunteer for the St John's Ambulance. Her father was a staunch Conservative and his strength of feeling put her off politics; although she felt a need to use her vote in order to show her support for the suffragettes who had fought so hard and suffered much to gain the vote for women. From there, she entered the civil service, and having passed her exams, and became a telegraphist. Her late husband Oscar was born in Balsall Heath and had a similar education. At 14, he left school and passed his exams to enter as a messenger boy, as Reg and Ken had. Oscar volunteered for active service and was trained as a wireless operator on planes for the RAF, but he had only just turned eighteen and a half when all the hostilities ceased. Consequently, he never saw any of the fighting.

On returning to the G.P.O. in 1947, he found that all the telegraphists had been moved upstairs, rather than, as Pat recalls, 'the bowels of the earth' that had been. She remembers that all the girls used to sit around a long table, and that's when she first saw Oscar, or should I say, Oscar's back. However, the girl next to her was quick to try and warn her off by saying:

"You don't want to go with him…he drinks."

Pat declares that she is very glad that she ignored this statement as she hardly saw him drink in his life. Their romance bloomed, and eventually they married in St Paul's church in Balsall Heath in 1950. Pat had five sisters, so her father was very grateful to start to see them married off.

Beryl Rose is the final lady left alive to tell her and her husband's story. Beryl was born in rural Cleobury Mortimer. Her grandfather died one day while hunting and left her mother some money. In those days, the man of the household controlled any finances of his wife, and so it was with Beryl's parents. Beryl's father decided to invest the money in building a house on Solihull Lane, Hall Green, Birmingham for £400, complete with garage and shed. He had been a travelling salesman for a Birmingham paint firm; unfortunately, the money ran out and so did he. Beryl's mother was a very pragmatic woman, and she bought a general store over in Lozells. Besides having a very small girl in Beryl, she also had another baby boy, and running a shop as well as all of the childcare meant that Beryl would stay with her cousins out towards Bridgenorth. As she recalls, it was a very primitive existence in the house in the back of beyond, with oil lamps and no electricity. During this time, Beryl would return during the long holidays to stay with her mother.

Beryl had a much older step-brother from her mother's first marriage. Eventually, the shop was given to him and a house was rented in Park Avenue for the small family: Beryl, her younger brother Roy and her mother. They had three quarters of the house where eventually my mother and father would rent a small flat. Beryl recalls that her brother Roy was always sickly, and he managed to contract tuberculosis of the lung and had to be sent to Switzerland for six months for the air.

It was when Beryl was 15 and staying with relatives back in Cleobury Mortimer, that she first met the man that would be her future husband. Norman Rose was born in Leopold Street in Balsall Heath where he grew up. His father died when Norman was young, forcing his mother to have to return to work. As a consequence, Norman brought up his younger brother, and his elder of the two sisters brought up her smaller sister. Beryl remembers them all with fond affection: a lovely family and very close. Norman was a Rover Scout and on a camp in Cleobury Mortimer. Beryl took a shine to him, and when she was out riding a horse she used to encourage him to take a ride on it. Norman had never ridden before, and Beryl

5. From little acorns...

had a mischievous streak, and used to smack the horse on the rear to make it go a bit faster than probably Norman would like.

On returning to Birmingham, Norman became a regular visitor to the shop, taking the tram from Balsall Heath and being made to sit on the crates of drinks in the shop by her mother; never allowed in the house. They were both young and Beryl was not ready at that point to settle down. Eventually, Norman had his call up, and entered the navy as an electrician, later becoming a Leading Torpedo Operator. Beryl's mother would not let her join the forces, so she passed her test to drive an ambulance for the civil defence; she says she liked the excitement of the wartime, everything was so different and less mundane. While Norman was away, Beryl met someone else who appealed more, as he had offered her a motorbike. A little while later, Beryl was invited to a party at the Rose's home by his sister. Norman was to be on leave and Beryl decided to go. She realised then that he was the one for her, and broke off the other relationship. They were married in January 1942 in St Alban's church in Balsall Heath. She continued to live with her mother in Park Avenue. She remembers my mother Margaret with fond affection:

"Pretty little thing she was... always reading books at the end of the garden."

They became close friends and remained so, until my mother died.

By the time Norman was demobbed in 1946, they had their first child: a daughter, Pam, and Beryl had rented a flat in Soho Road. Those were the tough times for everyone: austerity was biting, everything was rationed and queues formed everywhere. My own mother used to say, if you saw a queue, even if you did not know what it was for, you joined it. Beryl was only able to get a bed settee for the flat, and found it too difficult to live there, so they returned to her mother's home. Norman had returned to civilian life and was working as a carpenter. It was Beryl who first came across the advert in the local newspaper that Reg had placed seeking tradesmen for the scheme. Norman had the skills they needed and the young couple needed a home.

From left to right – (Row one) Figure 1 – Reg and Dot Harvey. Figure 2 – Harry Pestridge circa 1950. (Row two) Figure 3 – Pauline and Ken Quiney. Figure 4 – Pat and Oscar Rowson

From left to right – (Row one) Figure 5 – Norman Rose. Figure 6 - Beryl Rose. (Row two) Figure 7 – Margaret, Joseph, John, Alison and James Debney.

Chapter 6

Laying the foundations

It was Dot Harvey's mother that first planted the seed of the idea in the mind of Reg. As Reg recalls, she must have been getting a little fed up with her two daughters (and children) being in the house. She came across an article in a local newspaper about some Post Office workers who were looking to build their own homes. Reg speculates that this was probably the scheme that started at the Fordrough Lane depot amongst the workers there, the protagonist having been George Lavender. This scheme was eventually situated in two parts in Sheldon; it is considered by all to be the very first scheme of its kind to start but did not finish until much later and certainly after our scheme.

Reg began to think through the possibility of doing the same, but how to set about it and who to seek advice from evaded him at that stage. He was 21 years old, he had no building experience and no background in the trade, he was a civil servant and none of his family had any connections in the industry. Neither did any of his fellow workers. They were all approximately the same age, as they had been passed into the civil service in the annual batch of examinations and as a consequence formed their friendship groups accordingly. Reg began to informally discuss the possibility with one or two. Some would consider the whole idea 'pie in the sky', but he was very surprised at the positive reaction that others gave; if they were as desperate as Reg and Dot were, it was obvious why anyone might jump at the idea.

The young couple had tried, and tried, to get somewhere to rent, and by this stage their first daughter Tina had been born; every young family dreamed of their independence. They had come very close to renting a back-to-back at one point; anything was better than nothing, even if 14 families shared a court, lavatories and communal washing facilities. Despite existing legally-enforceable rent caps, landlords would find any way that they could to make extra money, and rental property was at a premium. The landlord insisted on key-money for this place for a settee that he had there: an exorbitant £200! When you consider that, at that time, Dot would have had to have stopped working because of the marriage bar, which prohibited employment for married women, and Reg, being 21, was on the lowest pay scale (only reaching the maximum ten years later), it was going to be an almost impossible task. Eventually, somehow Reg managed to raise the required sum through a friend of his father offering a loan. On returning to the 'gentleman' landlord, Reg found to his horror that it had already been let to someone for even more money. With so many still squatting in an around Birmingham, and landlords charging ridiculous additional money for terrible places that were gone in a flash, the younger people like Reg and Dot and the others at the G.P.O. had no hope of ever getting a place to live.

As Reg discussed his hair-brained idea in the canteen at work, it became more and more attractive to those that he talked to, and considerable enthusiasm was mounting. He knew he had to do some research, and the first obvious man to talk to was the head of the

6. Laying the foundations

Post Office workers' union in Birmingham, Bill Roach. This conversation proved to be of greatest value and Bill Roach was to become one of the biggest supporters for the venture. The unions had great sway with the labour government and had many contacts in Whitehall: it was not long before a telephone number was given to Reg of a man in the Ministry of Housing that he must talk to for guidance. Reg duly made the call, and has kept the handwritten note he made that day as the advice was given. It seems those that had discussed the notions of self-help four years previously, had formulated what they considered were the requirements for any brick-built, self-help scheme to be initiated. The man on the telephone was adamant for this idea to be at all possible that Reg needed to employ expertise: he would need some professional support to make the idea work. He advised Reg that he must secure the services of: a clerk of works (foreman), 2 electricians, 2 plumbers, 2 men for drains, 2 plasterers, 2 carpenters, 6 bricklayers, and 8 to 10 labourers. He further advised that external services would be required: an architect, a solicitor, an accountant, an administration clerk, transport and a mechanic. All Reg had at that time were some very keen telegraphists from the G.P.O., but he did have ambition and considerable entrepreneurial drive and thinking. Not daunted by this, he had an idea to advertise for the trades in the local press and to have half of the scheme as professionals, whilst he and the other Post Office workers could learn to be builders. Further conversations with Bill Roach were highly fruitful, and he then placed the idea with the Head Postmaster in Birmingham - Mr Sam Longford.

Reg was not the only keen and desperate young man to see the original article in the city press, others had caught sight of it too; the idea was catching fire. Most were employed working men in industry and big firms such as Joseph Lucas Ltd. When they approached their employees with a similar plan, they were not only met with the enthusiasm, but with offers of financial support. Unfortunately, being civil servants, the men from the G.P.O. could not seek any support other than that in kind; it is plausible to speculate that this had further impetus on how hard this particular group worked and how committed they were to achieve this, as they could not depend on cash hand-outs at any stage.

The initial 1936 housing legislation (referred to in chapter three), allowing housing associations to form, had been supplemented by a further Housing Act in 1949 (very much considered to be Nye Bevan's act). In this, there were provisions to take mortgages through the local authorities at a very favourable interest rate over 60 years, as long as these houses remained the property of the individual Local Authority in which they were built and could be rented to subsequent tenants. In other words, enabling housing associations to form and build council houses for the Local Authority and via the associations as landlords. How the men from G.P.O. set to organise their scheme at the end of 1950, paved the way for others to do likewise, by seeking their financial support in a more creative fashion.

It was within a very short space of time that the advert that Reg had speculatively placed in the evening press for 'professional tradesman wanted to build their own houses', bore fruit, quite significantly. They received 'sacksful' of mail and were completely inundated with desperate tradesmen, all wanting and willing to become involved. It so happens that one of the first applications by letter that he received was written by Harry, and having a very impressive 'C.V.' as Reg states, he knew that Harry had to be the first. Reg invited Harry to join, with the intention that Harry might teach the men from the G.P.O. and help select the professionals needed.

6. Laying the foundations

Reg had been to talk to the originator of the first G.P.O. scheme, the man featured in the article seen by Dot's mother. George Lavender, as we know, was still working as an engineer for the Post Office; eventually he was to attempt to set himself up as a self-styled consultant for self-help. According to Reg's understanding, prior to initiating the scheme in Tallington Road, George Lavender had trialled building a bungalow in Sheldon, Solihull on what was Lode Lane (later to become Old Lode Lane) near to Windsor Drive; I speculate based on my research subsequently, that the bungalow may have been built in tandem with the larger scheme. As the only way to build was subject to licence, he had found a disabled man who had priority for a licence and had convinced him to collaborate to see if it were possible to self-build. His networks of contacts were probably acquired through the main scheme: one of the principles being Shipway and Doble the local land agents (Mrs Doble had acquired considerable tracks all over the city and in Sheldon). George advised Reg that he would need to select a site, having formed his non-profit making association as a legal entity, and approach a Local Authority for licences (presuming of course that they could secure the finances). All was becoming clear in the mind of Reg how he had to proceed, and he needed to do several things simultaneously, as well as work at the same time. Dot and the other wives were always very active behind the scenes: in Dot's case, she became the unofficial administration clerk, organising letters, arranging appointments, keeping a check on what had to be done following their informal meetings and the other discussions that Reg was having. More importantly, she kept a check on the subscriptions that this newly formed group were making towards the building fund; they had considered that nominal contributions of a few pounds would suffice.

In the meantime, Reg and Harry began to go through the sacksful of mail looking for the best and most enthusiastic candidates: they both instinctively knew that these skills and character traits would be absolutely essential if this scheme was to be successful. Reg understood that, with his wartime leadership record, Harry was the best man to have oversight of the build itself. The selection and interview process took a little time; getting people together and making sure they had the skills needed. While this was coming together, the group from the G.P.O. met to keep the momentum of enthusiasm.

Eventually, they managed to pull together a team of 5 bricklayers (plus Harry): Len Crutchley, Horace Plume, Reg Smith (known as Baldy), Charlie Josebury, Jimmy Thompson, (later added to by George Spittle and Kenny Foster); carpenters: Sam Marfleet and Norman Rose; electricians: Harry Foster and Dan Ready; plumbers: Ken Robotham and Sid Steadman; drains: Jack Rogers; and a mechanic for the lorry, Reg Thorp. This was to add to the compliment of G.P.O. men already recruited as labourers; including: Ken Quiney, Oscar Rowson, Ron Mason, Bill Morgan, Jimmie Clayton, Bill Sterenberg (known as Dutchy), Jeff Walker (known as Jasper) Charlie Moseley, Denis Foster and Bob Roberts. There were three other members at the time, but attrition was common on these schemes either due to the financial or time commitments involved. They were replaced by others - first by George Spittle, a skilled bricklayer from the Black Country, and then in 1951 another labourer was added: Harry and Denis Foster's brother, Kenny.

As Dot fondly recalls, Dan Ready, one of the electricians, was the very last to be recruited from the newspaper advert. His future wife had refused to marry him unless he managed to get a house. He was so determined to get on the scheme according to Dot that he:

6. Laying the foundations

"Cycled all the way across Birmingham in the snow... He was so happy when we accepted him... He was such a nice man."

It was dawning on them all that the key external skills that they could not seem to find anywhere – without making a considerable investment for paid services out of the budget of their subscriptions – were the skills of an accountant. It was at that point that Norman Rose suggested my father. Norman had a lot to do with him, having lived at the same address, and was well aware that as a finance officer at a hospital, he knew all about drawing up sizeable cash flows and keeping very complex accounts. He also knew that my parents were in exactly the same position that everyone else was on the scheme: absolutely desperate for a home, with one child already dead and one living. Joe Debney came along to the meetings and was very quickly accepted, and he set to work organising the formalities of what was now becoming an official scheme.

The first formal meeting was held on the 7th August, 1950 at the Moseley Friends Institute. It was then that the ordered procedures for all further business were established under my father's guidance; it is in his handwriting that the first few sets of minutes are written. It was at this meeting that the first formal subscriptions were set out, at an initial deposit of £1, followed by weekly subscriptions of 2/6d weekly; this was very quickly revised thereafter when it became clear that this would not raise the required capital investment soon enough. It was decided to increase the subscriptions to £50 per family; £5 payable the beginning of September, £20 payable at the end of November and a further £20 payable at the end of March the following year

At these meetings, the officers and trustees were elected: Reg was duly elected secretary, as he had most of the contacts and had the drive to keep all of the external players informed and the ability to chase those that they still needed support from. My father was elected as treasurer, and was responsible for all the accounts and procurement of materials: raising orders, paying invoices etc. Ken Quiney, with his quiet and stable presence, was elected chairman and was very thorough in his role. As required by the law, they needed to form via a trust deed into an official association, and it was proposed at that first meeting to draft the trust deed. It is highly probable that George Lavender gave a contact of a solicitor that had helped the other G.P.O. scheme (A. C. Hayes, Sheppard and Padmore), and advised that, as they had experience drafting a trust deed for an association, it would be expedient to use them. It was probably the same advice by George Lavender that suggested the agents (Shipway and Doble) to help with securing land, and the architects (S. N. Cooke), for the design of the bungalow. It is possible to conclude that George Lavender proffered most advice at this stage, as there are connections to other data used on other schemes that link him as the advisor; the suggestion to make an approach to Bradford and Bingley Building Society may well have come from Mr Lavender too.

The scheme had to have a name, and that of the G.P.O. had already been used by the first scheme. It was on one of the many social outings that were arranged to try and keep the team together that Reg came up with the name. They were visiting Trentham Gardens as a group, and on their return journey on the bus they passed an avenue of silver birch trees. Reg was so taken with the picture that these trees made in the sunlight, that the name stuck and this housing association was christened 'The Silver Birch Housing Association'. My father took most of our shrubs and trees from the old gardener at Highcroft Hall, who went around breaking off twigs and shoots and advising him to put them in rooting powder and then straight in the ground. Indeed, we had a fine garden both front and rear, made up of an elm tree, a mountain ash tree, various hedges, roses, lilac and hydrangeas, but he was particularly proud of the four silver birch trees that he planted in a line on the very front boundary, which did not just dominate our garden; they seemed to dominate that end of the avenue.

The initial trust deed was drawn up by Mr Padmore the solicitor, for Evershed and Tompkinson Solicitors in Birmingham. My father, Reg, Harry and Ken were appointed the trustees of the association and all others who had then joined were listed. This document was signed and witnessed 7th November, 1950. It was updated the following year, 2nd July, 1951, when two members had left and two others replaced them. As Ken recalls, there were three that pulled out of the scheme: two because they were asked to leave as they were not maintaining the hours needed, and one who had a full refund of his contributions, as his wife had contracted MS. The responsibility fell on Ken's shoulders as the chairman to ask the two who had not applied their weight to leave.

Sam Longford was very enthusiastic for the idea and helped to facilitate their needs in kind. The first material support came via Bill Roach who offered places for them to meet and practice the skills that they would need. As the informal group, they had met where they could; at that time Bill Roach offered an old bombed out pub - The Samson and Lion, Hill Street - to hold their discussions and to begin to progress their plans. Once the meetings became formal they were held at the Moseley Friends Institute in Birmingham. Additionally, they were granted access to a garden at the back of a telephone exchange in Sandon Road in Bearwood; the proviso being that they did not walk through the exchange in their work boots.

So, the training sessions commenced in September 1950, at the telephone exchange. It was not a complete success, as Harry recalls, he was not happy with them trying to lay bricks:

"It took me seven years!"

However, what they lacked in technical skill, they more than made up for with their enthusiasm, and Harry persevered with his training, making them build courses in the back garden in Sandon Road and knocking them down again. They were painfully slow, and their work would never pass muster for any externally visible walls, but in order to retain their enthusiasm, while the trades were being recruited and to help to bond a team together, Reg pushed for regular sessions of learning to be brickies.

In those first meetings, great care was taken to plan and organise: a great deal of the success and speed of their completion can be attributed to how careful and dedicated these men were. It started with their planning: everything became subject to consideration and order. They were already discussing the type of house they could build based on the limitations of the possible rent that they could raise from their members. The women were consulted very early on in these discussions as to their thoughts on how this home should be configured, particularly arrangements in the kitchen; consideration was even given as to whether they should cook with gas or electric, as is clear from the minutes that they were offered both.

In these early discussions, they laid out the ground rules and expectations of the members of the association. They considered a proposal that every man should work 20 hours a week on the site (this would increase), and that only exceptions of sickness should be made allowances for. In the case of temporary absence through illness, a doctor's note had to

6. Laying the foundations

be provided and shown to the committee. As a mark of the social care and consideration of that time, it was considered essential that if any member were to become incapacitated through an accident or illness, his fellow members would rally around to undertake his share; even if that meant that each member left had to work additional hours.

Three fundamental things needed to happen for these grand plans to be turned into a possible reality: land had to be found, finance to build raised, and, crucially, the building licence for each bungalow acquired. All three of these factors were enormous in their undertaking, and each had to be addressed urgently. They were all to some extent mutually dependent on each other; you could not build without a licence, you could not get a licence unless you had land to build on, and without finance you could not afford to purchase the necessary building materials. The £50 contributed by each member eventually by March 1951 may have raised one pair of semi-detached bungalows (purchasing all the materials, plant and equipment for that build), but it would not cover the other 13 needed to build dwellings to house a further 26 families; a mortgage had to be raised from somewhere.

Equally, land had to be found. Reg was chasing a site to build on, but then, a licence was needed from the authority in which the land was situated, as well as essentially someone to borrow the money from to make all of this dreaming a reality. At the same time, he had to keep the enthusiasm and commitment going in a group of people who were, by now, a mixture between civil servants and trades, with no common ground other than that they wanted to build their own home out of sheer necessity. This was an immense juggling act for anyone, especially when you consider that Reg was still only twenty-two: quite an achievement for someone so young to manage to keep all these things going, and hold down a full-time job in the civil service with a young child as well.

At first, Reg was made an offer of a site in Northfield; both he and Dot would have quite liked Northfield, close to their respective kith and kin. However, within a few months they were offered a second site in Sheldon, Solihull; neither of them knew the area and decided to take the long bus ride out to view the site. Tina was a little tot at the time, Dot recalls. They took a picnic, and afterwards lay the little girl to sleep under a hedge to shade her from the afternoon sun. Despite his own personal ease of location and familiarity of the first offer of a site, Reg knew that he must be democratic, and the whole group had to be consulted and the proposals had to be put to a vote. As he remembers, it was 26:2 in favour of the Sheldon, Solihull site. Democracy had to be respected, and that site had been chosen, so application was made to Solihull UDC as whether the group might be able to build. At the same time, they applied for 30 licences to build; as several more associations chased hard on their heels doing the same, Silver Birch Housing Association were not the only interested party seeking somewhere to build.

Other groups were springing up all over the city, all trying to catch the wave of support at the same time. It is noted in the Solihull UDC Housing Committee minutes of mid-1950 that both Lucas and Dunlop had formed housing associations and had approached Solihull for building licences. However, the Council were concerned that any issue of licences might be 'debited' to the UDC and they had entered into discussions with central government to broker a deal whereby they could be issued additional licenses over and above their allocation in order to help these housing associations.

By early October 1950, Solihull had been promised consideration for additional licences the following spring. This raised further concerns that, as it was only a

6. Laying the foundations

'consideration' and nothing had been agreed, and because of the increasing difficulties nationally of sourcing materials, this decision 'might well be withdrawn'. Solihull were persistent in their discussions and two months later, they were promised 125 licences, as long as they continued to meet their targets for existing homes and completions, and 25 of those could be 'mortgaged'. Further, that a special provision could be 'agreed in principle' for the four housing associations that had requested to build in the Ebrington Avenue and Charingworth Road area, a total of 199 houses; as yet these licences were not available. Those four housing associations were: Silver Birch, which had requested 28 licences; 'U-Build-It' (Lucas), which had requested 38 licences; Sparkhill, which had requested 40 licences; and Tyburn, which had requested 12 licences. It is also noted in the Housing Committee minutes of early December 1950, that a 'central organisation' was being formed to have oversight of the various groups activities; it appears George Lavender had begun to consider himself as the man to co-ordinate a self-styled Midlands organisation for self-help.

There was a general feeling that, if the Conservatives would be returned at the second General Election within the next twelve months (the previous General Election of 1950 had only returned Labour with a slim majority), the restrictive licensing laws for building would be in some way made more flexible, to enable greater headway towards the impossible housing targets. If, as an association, a group of men could build a house for an authority, they could supplement the council housing stock, and thus use licences in a Local Authority where manpower may be in short supply, such as Solihull (in effect increasing the availability of licences), or add to numerous building schemes for council houses around Birmingham (and effectively supplement the manpower needed without additional cost). At the same time, every promise of four council houses in an authority would trigger one license for a private build for a Local Authority, Solihull was particularly interested in this prospect, as it had people waiting to make private builds, but they were unable to secure licences. In the Housing Committee Minutes (6/12/50) the Council acknowledge that:

"It would appear, therefore that the Council stood to benefit by the arrangements in that they could get additional houses for private licences."

This whole quid pro quo situation could be mutually-beneficial to all of the parties involved, as long as licences became available. This is where the first and most significant problem arose. Although licences were at the disposal of local authorities – it was only at their discretion as to which council housing project they were distributed to, or (in the case of the few private licences) which client they were issued to – these licences were ultimately controlled by the regional distribution committee, who in turn had their licences rationed from central government. With building materials and manpower so short nationally, and some areas drastically falling behind on their building targets, Whitehall had seen fit to restrict licences in areas where performance was very good in order to redirect them where the problems were; assuming that any shortfall in labour could be made up by travelling contractors. Additionally, both Birmingham and Solihull were only too aware of how effective this solution could be and were keen to support self-help (after all, there had been these mutterings coming from central government five years before to support the lot of the self-helper). However, there were quite a few hopeful housing associations chasing pieces of land and licences all at that same moment, probably due to the same article that Dot's mother had first raised Reg's attention to. It was obvious to both authorities, Birmingham and Solihull, that with a possible change of government so close, and not really knowing which

6. Laying the foundations

way the wind was going to blow politically, an element of caution had to be taken until things became clearer. What they must not do is allow these enthusiastic young men to lose their will to try, but no promises could be given at that moment, other than vague murmurs of support, and any scarce licences that did become available would have to be rationed.

Meanwhile, having written to a few building societies and having had no response, Reg was overjoyed when the Bradford and Bingley Building Society showed interest. This is the same society the George Lavender was known to use; as to whether he had paved the way or if the BBBS was independently inspired to support self-build remains unclear. My father and Reg were invited to lunch at the Queen's Hotel in Birmingham by the building society, they were very impressed with the way they were treated, and the offer made was very reasonable. The Bradford and Bingley made it very clear that they would not loan anything until they had the first pair of semi-detached bungalows built up to damp-proof course level, and the building society had inspected it and found it to be satisfactory. If it passed muster then they would release 10% of the total value of that bungalow; the scheme would then receive four more stage payments for the value of the bungalow to each respective level; top of window, top of wall, roof on, all fitments in. This process would then apply to each group of bungalows (licenses having been issued) for each stage. As it was more than likely that the building society's final valuation would far outstrip the estimated build costs, all seemed very favourable indeed. Still, during those dark winter months as 1950 turned to 1951, no approval was given to build, never mind acquire licenses; yet still the group met for training and persevered with their planning.

They knew that they needed vital pieces of equipment: some sort of heavy transport, a site hut, scaffolding, the necessary spades, picks and shovels. This sort of equipment might be commonly available in the industrial-based associations that were forming, or in some cases, might even have been purchased for them, but the civil servants knew that, because of restrictions on what they could have, they would have to be far more creative and resourceful.

George Lavender seems to have become equally enterprising, and according the minutes, had offered scaffolding poles, putlogs and chains at costs to the association (these were initially accepted in principle, however other solutions were found in the meantime). The G.P.O. had its own fleet of heavy lorries, as Reg recalls, that used to reach end of life (where service costs outstripped the value of retaining that vehicle); some vehicles were in much better condition than most when they came up for resale. It just so happened that one such 30 CWT, Morris, Commercial lorry became available in very good condition, which the association managed to acquire for 57/ 10; quite reasonable when you realise that they eventually re-sold it for more than they paid for it when the scheme was over. Sam Longford offered the shovels, forks, spades, and picks at nominal costs, and old telegraph poles as putlogs (cross pieces on scaffolding). This saved a shilling or two being spent elsewhere.

Still they waited for news. All was an act of faith for every member of that group. They had formed an association, invested a substantial amount of money each, which most would have struggled to find. They were challenged by their own lack of skills and expertise in areas that were not in their personal sphere of knowledge and understanding. They were all Birmingham men but now were crossing the border into a different authority, which as yet would not agree to let them build, never mind issue the first licence for the advantage of only two of the families in that scheme. Would the rest of those families, whose menfolk would invest their 20 hours a week as extra work, benefit in the long run? What about the money?

6. Laying the foundations

Would they get one of the five stage-payments from the building society, never mind all five? Would their work be good enough? Harry was trying teach men to build who had never built in their lives before. Harry also knew, as a foreman and clerk of works, that materials were at a premium if available at all. He must have been full of many doubts at that time, though he may never have expressed them. Reg had everything on his shoulders: if all succeeded 28 families would have homes; if all failed, 28 families would have invested a great deal of time, effort and money. The worry for Reg and the sense of responsibility that lay on him in January of 1951 must have been enormous.

6. Laying the foundations

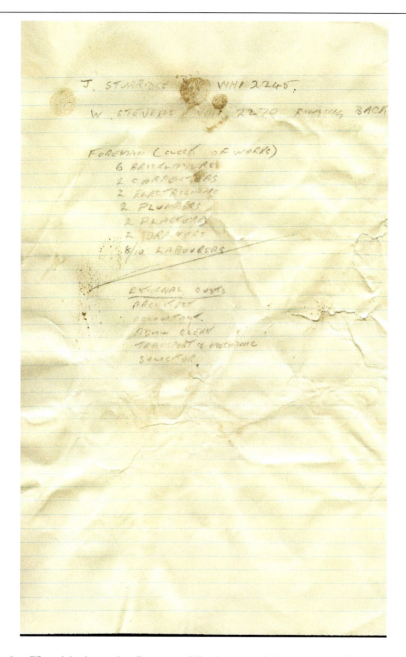

Figure 8 – The original note that Reg wrote following the call from the 'man from the Ministry'.

Stamp
10s.

Ext with
Orgd in own
power
Everchell&
TrentRowan
Solrs
Moorland Hse
6 St Charles St
B'ham 3

8th April 1957.

THIS TRUST DEED made the 7th day of November 1950 BETWEEN HARRY PESTRIDGE and Others whose names addresses and occupations are set forth in the Second Schedule hereto (hereinafter called "the Members") of the one part and REGINALD NORMAN HARVEY of 263 Shenley Fields Road Selly Oak Birmingham KENNETH JESSE QUINEY of 97 Daw End Lane Rushall Walsall and JOSEPH WILLIAM DEBNEY of 12 Park Avenue Handsworth Birmingham (hereinafter called "the Trustees") of the other part

WHEREAS:-

(1) The Members are desirous of forming themselves into an association for the purpose of erecting 28 dwelling-houses for their own individual occupation and with the view thereto each have agreed to contribute voluntarily his own work and labour in the erection of all the said houses and to establish a building fund of £1260 by the subscription thereto of the sum of Forty-five pounds each for the purpose of the purchase of all the initial materials and equipment necessary for the construction of the said dwellinghouses.

(2) In furtherance of the said desire the Members have agreed to acquire freehold and/or leasehold lands in the Counties of Warwickshire and/or Worcestershire upon which the Members intend to erect detached or semi-detached bungalows and/or houses after necessary licenses have been obtained.

(3) At a meeting of the Members held at The Post Office Welfare Centre Hill Street Birmingham on the Third day of September 1950 under the Chairmanship of the said Kenneth Jesse Quiney it was unanimously resolved as follows:-

 (i) That it was expedient that all land acquired for the purposes of the said Association and the moneys subscribed by Members as aforesaid and all other the moneys of the Association shall be vested in Trustees.

 (ii) That the Trustees should be Trustees for the purposes of holding the said land and the moneys subscribed by the Members and other moneys as aforesaid

Figure 9 – The Trust document, signed by the four trustees; Reg, Ken, Joe and Harry.

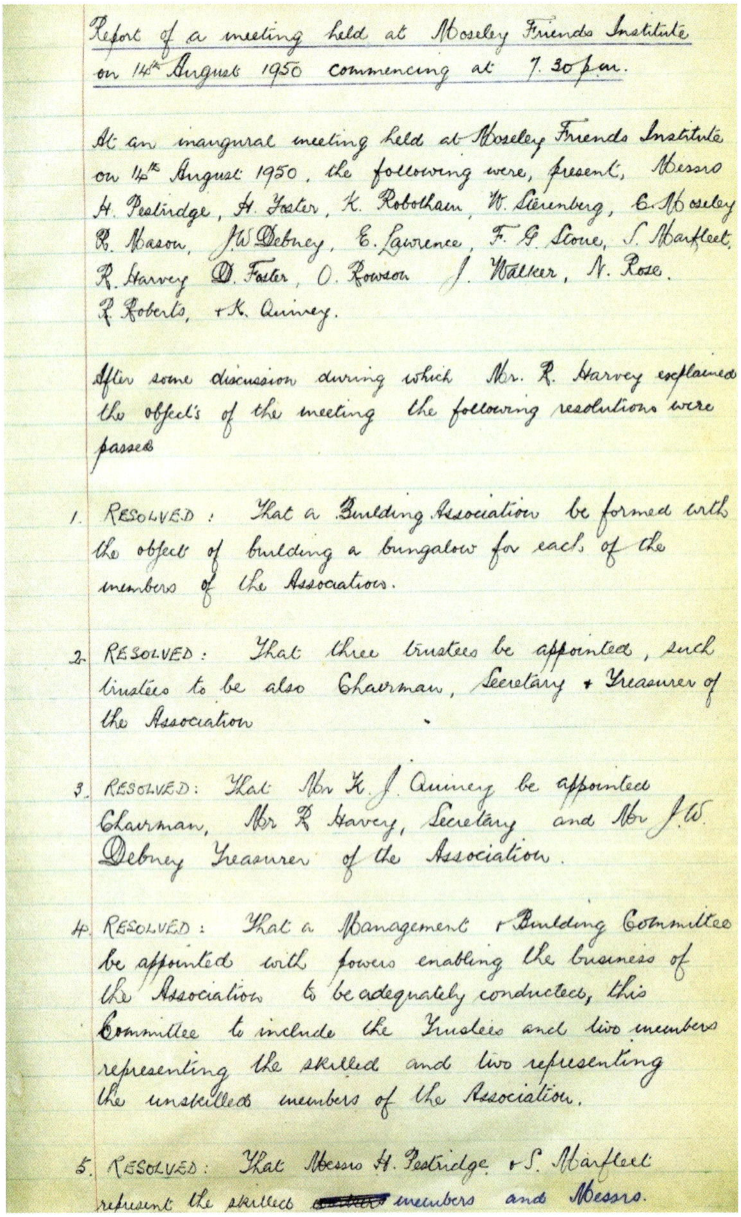

Report of a meeting held at Moseley Friends Institute on 14th August 1950 commencing at 7.30 p.m.

At an inaugural meeting held at Moseley Friends Institute on 14th August 1950, the following were present. Messrs H. Pestridge, H. Foster, K. Robotham, W. Sterenberg, E. Moseley, R. Mason, J.W. Debney, E. Lawrence, F.G. Stone, S. Harfleet, R. Harvey, D. Foster, O. Rowson, J. Walker, N. Rose, R. Roberts, & K. Quiney.

After some discussion during which Mr. R. Harvey explained the objects of the meeting the following resolutions were passed

1. RESOLVED: That a Building Association be formed with the object of building a bungalow for each of the members of the Association.

2. RESOLVED: That three trustees be appointed, such trustees to be also Chairman, Secretary & Treasurer of the Association

3. RESOLVED: That Mr K. J. Quiney be appointed Chairman, Mr R. Harvey, Secretary and Mr J.W. Debney Treasurer of the Association.

4. RESOLVED: That a Management & Building Committee be appointed with powers enabling the business of the Association to be adequately conducted, this Committee to include the Trustees and two members representing the skilled and two representing the unskilled members of the Association.

5. RESOLVED: That Messrs H. Pestridge & S. Harfleet represent the skilled members and Messrs.

Figure 10 – The first set of minutes for the scheme written by my father Joseph William Debney.

6. Laying the foundations

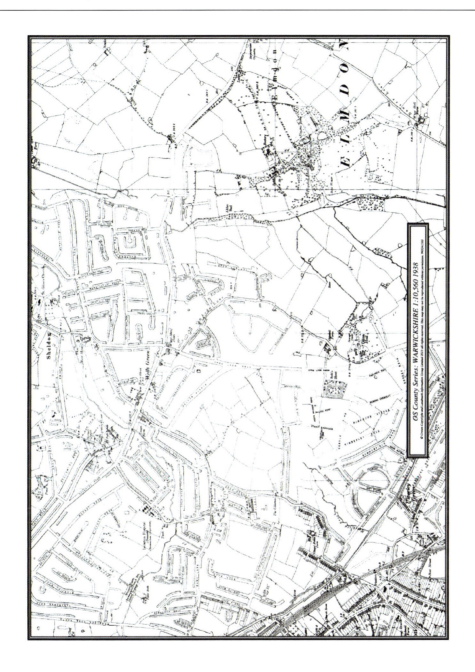

*Figure 11 – Map 1938 showing the rural location of the unnamed Ebrington Avenue.
"With grateful thanks to www.old-maps.co.uk and Ordnance Survey for allowing me to reproduce this image"*

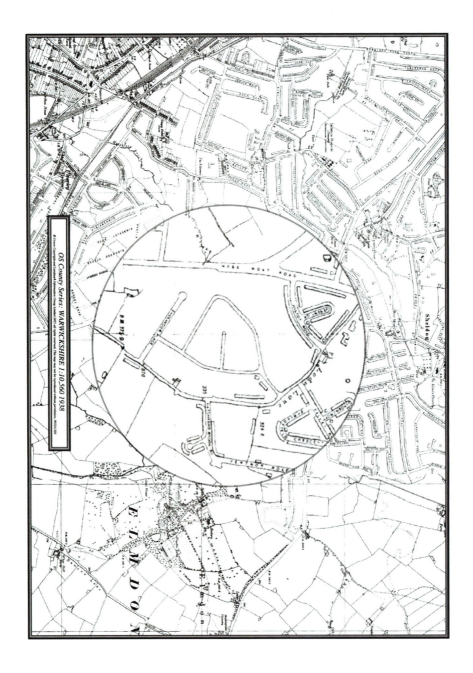

Figure 12 – A section enlargement of 1938 map showing; Ebrington Avenue, Charingworth Road and Glenside Avenue. "With grateful thanks to www.old-maps.co.uk and Ordnance Survey for allowing me to reproduce this image."

Figure 13 – The ex-GPO Lorry.   Figure 14 – The Ebrington Avenue site.

Figure 15 – The site hut and the marking out of plots. Figure 16 – Digging, digging, digging – drains!

Chapter 7

Brick by brick

Early April 1951, the tide had begun to turn in their favour. It is recorded in the minutes of the association that Solihull had finally given the group permission to move onto the Sheldon site. The planning approval had been passed through Building, Plans and Town Planning on the 2nd April for the first four associations who wanted to start building in Solihull, and all geographically located together. All of the bungalows appear to be of similar designs, yet they are significantly different, however they were all designed by the same firm of architects.

The design used by Silver Birch was drawn up by S. N Cooke and Partners, a firm of architects based in Birmingham. As George Lavender is copied into all correspondence as regards planning at that stage, in his capacity as General Secretary for the Central Advisory Committee for Self-Help (operating out of the offices of Shipway and Doble) it appears that he was already being considered somewhat of an expert by the Council. He is certainly mentioned in later minutes of the Housing Committee as having an association with four out of the five original schemes, of which Silver Birch was one. From the interviews, we do know that Silver Birch did not seek the support of Mr Lavender's group and proceeded to operate independently. This independence from an interceding group may have been a further reason why they finished before any others did; fewer governing bodies involved, less red-tape and less expenditure to another body.

Finally, Silver Birch could put all of their plans could into action. As they all had discussed at the previous meetings, the first priority was to create a secure place to keep all of the tools, equipment and materials that they would need to purchase as they went along. This space would need to hold enough resources for an on-going project of potentially 14 pairs of semi-detached bungalows; there maybe be 2 to 10 or so in construction at any one time. The scaffolding poles that they had purchased from George Lavender, the various items of equipment and tools from the G.P.O.; all would have to be stored under lock and key. This building would have to accommodate a great deal. In the minutes, it is decided that Harry would seek a supply of second-hand bricks for this purpose: having his position and access to his vast network of contacts in and around the city, Harry Pestridge was in the best placed position to do this. In that meeting, they organised into two groups; one to attend the site and commence building the site hut, and the other to attend the Sandon Road training as normal.

It was 8th April when the team first set foot on the Ebrington Avenue site; a far cry from the view that you get today. Ken Quiney remembers the excitement he felt as he changed into some old trousers and boots and took the trolley bus for the fifteen-minute bus ride from the 'centre of town' (Birmingham), along the Coventry Road; you could not travel the same distance these days in less than three quarters of an hour with all of the congested

7. Brick by brick

traffic. The whole area had been farm land; in fact, where my parents' house was to be sited there was a swamp-like area, very likely an old pond. As a child, I was fascinated by the many frogs and toads that inhabited our garden; not a normal little girl by any description. I would spend countless hours making frog friends, and, being the creatures they were, they would return year on year to the same areas. I became very adept at identifying the same characters as they passed through our rather boggy garden.

It was such a rural idyll – that those interviewed have noted – the very different life they had at that time, in comparison to the present day. Joan Pestridge says that you used to be able to pick blackberries where the doctors became situated, and the country farm still existed on Lode Lane. It was not without its war scares either. As Harry pointed out, there had been an Ack Ack site at the top of Lode Lane, obviously, that would have left some debris and encouraged the occasional flak from passing German bombers. In fact, 'a stick of bombs' as Harry remarked, fell just on the edge of what was the build, at the area we all knew locally as the gully.

The land was owned by a Mr Jack Cotton, a local landlord of some note, possessing many pieces of land over a considerably-sized area. The site of Olton End Farm, had been the prior occupants of what was now to be the Silver Birch Housing Association Site. Up to that point you could see for miles across fields and hedges, however, there were three or four other associations actively seeking land in the same area. It was not going to be long before multiple little building sites of furious activity would spring up at all the odd hours of the day and night. The only marks on this otherwise rural vista were the bare concrete strips of road that had been laid. Rumour has it amongst the scheme members that these roads had been laid by Italian prisoners of war during the war years. However, on an O.S. map of 1938, there are clear indications that a road had been laid but, as of that date, was unadopted. It certainly makes more sense that this road was over 12 years in age, as all that arrived describe the potato plants growing through the laid surface.

In fact, the likelihood that the road had been laid for much longer than a few years is further evident from the flood-pond that awaited our 'would-be builders' on the first day that they arrived. Years of continual farming of the land since the road had been laid (and that much-needed food production during the war – hence the potatoes), had caused an enormous amount of silt and mud to be washed onto the rough surface. The storm drains that were part of the road-build had become blocked, causing all the water to pool on the surface, and laying quite deep. It was at this point that Ken realised the enormity of the task they were facing: as he said, it was that sudden realisation of the reality 'what have we done?' According to Ken, the first thing that Harry had to do was find a very long pole, and go the full length of the road finding the gutter's edge and poking to locate the drains to let the water go. A mixture of the stagnant water and rotting potato crops leads to a very interesting aroma: a pungent smell that the men bitterly complained about for the first few weeks. Mounds of rotten potatoes lay on the sides of the roads, stinking and cooking as the weather began to warm up.

Although the drainage was there, and there was a mains connection of the electrical supply to the site, there were no footpaths or street lights, this was a very bare, mainly muddy vista. The road was just roughly laid concrete sections, no final metal added to complete the surface: this would be a bone-of-contention for many years later, why Solihull never finished the road with tarmac. But that is another story, much further on than this tale.

7. Brick by brick

The placement of the site hut was decided by its proximity to the mains connection, obviously staying only on that land allocated to Silver Birch, for any contravention of the planning permission at this stage could cause the whole project to cease. Silver Birch Housing Association were going to be scrutinised closely, and every action that they did as perceived amateurs, would be monitored and measured. The adjacent self-build operations for the other self-help associations, Lucas, Sparkbrook, Tyburn and 'U Build It', were quite literally next door on all sides, so there was no room for error and the site marks for each plot had to be adhered to.

The site of the hut was also determined by the start of the build; it made no sense to build this hut on land that they were going to use for the first five pairs, it had to be the site of the fourteenth pair. As it happens, this was the site of Ken Quiney's house, as he was the last man in, in 1953: the twenty-eighth and final bungalow. The site hut tuned out to have a bigger footprint than any of the bungalows, and with the team of expert bricklayers, a mound of purchased second-hand bricks, offloaded from the back of the purchased ex- G.P.O. lorry, the team set to work. They had the whole thing up in a day, remarkably, and the roof on. As Ken remembers it was up and running in 24 hours with a toilet around the back, and Dickie Foster having made the connection to the mains for the floodlights. This was going to be the start of a long, hard twenty-eight months for them all, working their additional twenty hours on top of their working week, many travelling long distances to do so, in all weathers: in the long, hot days of two summers, and under artificial light in the darkness over two hard winters. No holidays would be asked for or granted; the only day off that would be allowed would be Christmas Day.

The first spades went in the ground that April, and it was all about digging! Digging trenches for drains and sewers, digging trenches for footings. The soil around there had a clay base and probably flooded frequently, so as fast as they dug, if trenches were left open to the rain overnight or during the day, they probably spent a considerable amount of time bailing-out too. They had formulated their plan so that all hours were covered, and those that worked more accommodating hours, such as the men from the G.P.O. with their shift pattern, could cover times when the men from the trades were working. As the civil servants lacked the skills, they became the labourers, and digging became their role. In order to cover their individual 20 hours' expectation weekly, each man had to work three evenings each week, Saturday afternoons (after they had finished their paid work) and all day each Sunday. The G.P.O. shifts allowed for many of these men to attend the site from 4pm every day, which would allow a considerable amount of labouring, site clearing, and unloading to be done before the trades arrived: it lent itself to a much more efficient system of operations.

What would become clear from the outset, was that this intelligent solution to recruit half of the scheme as tradesmen would pay very big dividends for this housing association. While other schemes started before them, and may have had far more men, and/or considerable financial support from their employers, what they lacked were the skilled personnel: it was not unusual to find a scheme of thirty or forty men with only one qualified bricklayer, for instance. Silver Birch, on the other hand, had a team of 5 bricklayers; 6 if you included Harry Pestridge who was a fully trained. By all accounts it was a superlative team! Jimmy Thompson was one of the fastest bricklayers most had ever seen; he used a wetter mix, and could build precision walls at great speed. These were men that 'worked on the lump' as it was called in their professional lives; it meant they got paid for a quoted price for work done, and they could work extremely quickly as a result. The main result of all this incisive recruitment and planning was that there was going to be no wasted time: this scheme was destined to finish as soon as possible, with the consequence that it would be an unremitting slog.

As the 'man from the Ministry' had first advised Reg, he would need a man for drains: Silver Birch had Jack Rogers, assisted by Ron Mason. As Jack insisted from the outset, being an engineer for the Post Office, he could dig a drain better than anyone. Drain digging requires a certain amount of skill to ensure: one, that the trench is deep enough; and two, that the level of the drain allows for a slight incline down to the main sewer, and that when the ceramic pipes (as they were then) are laid, that they are correctly supported so as not be stressed to fracture. Jack's oversight of all this was critical. Foundations and drains were the invisible but critical underpinning of everything.

Solihull was not just going to allow anything to proceed unchecked, especially at this critical early stage. It was a whole new venture for the authority to have this explosion of self-builders suddenly arrive, all wanting land at one and the same moment, all wanting licences to build at exactly the same time. The Council had to act on faith too; they had no idea which schemes would be most productive, experience fewer or more problems, lack skill or have those skills in abundance. The only fact that the Council could guarantee was that each of these schemes was absolutely committed to giving the best damn shot that they could. They had found the money as each individual investor (probably against the odds and in tough circumstances), the vast majority had absolutely no skills to speak of, and yet, they were going to attempt to build their own homes; and not just one or two, but at that moment, one or two hundred.

As much as Solihull would have loved this to be an absolute success from the outset, there were just too many unknown factors. The UDC would have to tread very carefully, after all, it had its own interests to consider. It was in the process of applying for a charter of incorporation; to be subsequently assessed as not diligent in their undertakings (as being wasteful with its financing, or neglectful with its regulation), would not have stood that application in good stead. Added to that, there were only so many licenses available. Although the Labour government had begun to see that these few self-helpers may indeed help the national targets, they were still highly restrictive with the issue of licences at a national level, leaving regional areas with the difficult task of apportioning on a local level to each Local Authority, who in turn, could each plead a deserving case for preferential treatment.

With all these competing pressures and interests in mind, when Solihull had finally agreed to issue licences to Silver Birch, it was only for 10 in the first instance. As a consequence, and because no one at that stage knew definitively how they were going to nominate families to houses, it must have left all feeling very uncertain, though elated that they were finally getting somewhere. Yet again, all was not straightforward: the group knew that the release of funds on the block mortgage was dependent on an inspection up to damp-proof course on the first pair of bungalows. This would mean that, in order to buy the remaining materials for the other 4 pairs (8 semi-detached bungalows), they would need to concentrate on that one first. Also, Solihull Planning department wanted to ensure that its faith was not being misplaced; they required the scheme to submit planning notices at each

7. Brick by brick

stage of the build process; the first stage would be those very first trenches. It was of even greater importance that Jack Roger's advice was followed to the letter.

Consideration had to be given by the Silver Birch members as to how these first houses should be allocated. It was decided to adopt the same strategy that prioritised council houses; those with greatest need in first - those with children. Most of the men on the scheme were newly married and were just starting families, except in a very few cases such as Ken Quiney who was not married as yet, and so those men were at the back of the queue. My own parents would have had two children by then, but for the sad fact that my elder sister had died; they, like nine other families, had one child each. Ken and Margie Robotham had three children, Jimmy and Jean Clayton had two children, and everyone else had yet to start their families. It was decided that, as the expertise and leadership were vital to the on-going success, Harry and Joan Pestridge should take the very first house that was finished. As foreman, it was imperative that he was there. In the other half of that first pair, it would be Mr and Mr Robotham, as they had three children. Then, when the scheme could move to build the next 8 licences, the first of those would go to Mr and Mrs Clayton and then the following would be drawn by lots of all those families with one child.

As Reg recalls, the ballot between the families with one child was quite a nerve-racking affair. All nine names with one child were placed in a hat, and then those drawn out would be allocated those licences in order. At that stage, there were seven remaining licences and nine families (plus all those without children waiting for more licences they hoped to made available). Reg says that the nerves got to him so much that he stood outside. He was very glad that he had, as his name was called first: being the originator of the scheme and the secretary, it may have looked like a rigged ballot had he been in the room. Nine names were called out in order; Harvey, Smith, Josebury, Crutchley, Roberts, Marfleet, Morgan, Thorp and then Debney. My parents and their neighbours (Reg and Ann Thorp), would have to wait along with the other expectant hopefuls that all their hard work to help ten other families would amount to something permanent for themselves. This time of waiting was an act of trust for many, and the ballot was not without some controversy amongst the members later that year.

There was a long way to go before they could start to lay bricks for the first pair of bungalows, as Reg had submitted the first planning notice for Solihull to inspect those carefully dug trenches. The Solihull surveyor came along with a small team of men and proceeded to conduct a very antiquated (according to Harry) test of trench density, which consisted of setting up a scaffold and gantry over the trench, then dropping a heavy weight at various points along its length to see how far that became embedded in the ground. In Harry's opinion, it was because they had not had to use more modern methods available at that time, and they simply did not know any other way of testing. However, to the relief of all, particularly Reg, the trenches passed and they were able to proceed to the all critical 'laying of the foundations and the first building up to damp-proof course', as stipulated by the Bradford and Bingley Building Society.

Under Harry's watchful eye all proceeded carefully and in a very disciplined way. Step-by-step, those with limited skill were guided as to what they were required to do. My father had managed to negotiate a special rate with the Stonebridge Brick Company of all their fire-damaged bricks; not the most perfect red brick that all would have liked, as they had a bluish colouring to them, but they were good for the lower part of walls, or on internal walls to be plastered. Many would say now that the ones that can be seen give a very individual 'hand-made' brick finish to those bungalows; it was an economic measure that saved money for the scheme.

When the time came to inspect the necessary stage by the building society it was passed without comment, as Ken says:

"If these places weren't any good, we'd never have got the money."

The scheme could breathe a bit. With the excellent valuation that the building society had placed on the end result, and the advance of those first monies, they were able to build to the next stage and the next without stress, as well as laying the drains and foundations for the other 8 licences.

With the skills of Len Crutchley, Charlie Josebury, Reg Smith, Horace Plume, and of course Jimmy Thompson all building with skill and precision, it was not long until they were up to top of window, top of wall and roof height on the first pair. Now this is where all those training sessions and talks that had happened during those months of waiting paid off: those with trades applied their skills to the mounting number of tasks, those without laboured intensively on-site clearance and preparation for the other eight licences, and there was always digging, lots of digging! One of the talks given during the early training had been Sam Marfleet, explaining the roof construction. Now it all began to make sense in the larger scale, and every man seemed to know where their individual contribution applied in the list of tasks to do. Reg was on trenches, and after they had been dug he had to peg out every six foot and level, always measuring correctly for the proper ground elevation as set by the architect to one specific point on the site; Harry, not one for letting things slip, would always check. Harry was known for always double-checking everything; absolutely nothing was left to chance.

Materials acquisition and purchase was always going to pose a problem; the supplies of timber were particularly difficult to source. Everything had to be carefully accounted for, and nothing could allow an overstretch of the limited capital: if a material could not be bought because of the shortness of supply, an alternative had to be found. I often wondered why we had metal internal door frames and skirting boards; the supply of timber was so critical that metal was the only alternative. We were lucky that our window frames were in wood, as it was the case that other schemes in our vicinity had to opt for metal for these as they had no other alternative.

Finally, the roof had to be tiled. The scheme had opted for a dreadnought clay tile for durability and they planned to tile it themselves. None of the trades were roofers, but they knew enough to do the job very well, if very slowly; it took considerably longer than for skilled tilers to complete. However, as Ken noted, everything had to be inspected meticulously by Solihull UDC, and in order to proceed with the next four pairs of bungalows, a final planning notice for the first build had to be presented by Reg in order that a surveyor could make a site visit and check that all was in order with the build.

Unfortunately, despite the tile being of a very superior quality and deemed to last considerably longer than any alternative that may be suggested, the surveyor refused to pass the roof, stating that the tiles were not in keeping with the area and other sand-faced concrete tiles would have to be applied. Although annoying that it would have to be re-tiled, this decision was of benefit to the scheme. Once my father had worked out the quantities and costs involved in applying all of the roofs (with the time to do so factored in by members of the scheme applying the tiles) and then compared that against the cost of employing a sub-contractor to do all, it was far more cost-effective to choose the latter solution.

There were still four other pairs of bungalows being built. There was no time for slacking, and it was the first winter: the nights would soon be drawing in, the floodlights would be up and running and the weather would not be forgiving. Meanwhile, some of those families that had not been in the ballot were agitated by the lack of any communications from Solihull as to the issue of the remaining licences, and began to question why the ballot had been conducted just for those who had children, as it was in their considerations a discretionary act that the scheme could allocate in any way they saw fit. This had been the rumour circulating from the three other schemes who were also now engaged in feverish building activity close by. The Silver Birch trustees (Reg, Ken and Joe) insisted that they had followed the national guidance for allocation on social need and that remained the most equitable and fair method of deciding who would be in first.

As predicted by many, the Conservatives were returned to government in November of 1951, with Winston Churchill once again as PM. The highly dependable Harold Macmillan had been appointed as the Minister for Housing. The Tories had swept to victory by promising to deliver the houses that their predecessors had failed to build and more. In a country still suffering the grip of austerity, and so many still homeless, the change of leadership of the country was inspiring, and Winston Churchill was perceived nationally as the wartime leader who had got things done. In order for Macmillan to understand where the shortages in housing needs were, and where the resources had to be targeted, a suspension of licensing followed to allow a stock-taking process to be done.

This could not have come at a worse time for Reg and the Silver Birch scheme, as they had an outstanding application for the other eighteen licences. Added to this, the idea of self-help was taking off, with many schemes forming over the border in Birmingham, and when land was not being made available there, they were making their approaches to Solihull.

As licences were limited by authority and came out of a yearly allocation and were already in short supply, there were real fears that these remaining licences would be spread too thin among those schemes currently building; those in the planning stage; and those waiting. The members of Silver Birch had to carry on in blind faith that all would come good. Following countless inspections and close scrutiny, they managed to complete the first pair: 72 and 70 Ebrington Avenue. Harry and Joan Pestridge and their daughter moved in just before Christmas, in plenty of time for Harry to keep a watchful eye out on the site and all of the workmanship. Ken and Margie Robotham and their three children moved in January 1952. A new year and a new start for two young families; but the long slog to finish the rest stretched out before every member of the scheme, and there were still eighteen licences outstanding.

Figure 17 & 18 – Laying the hard pads: everything was done with the most basic of tools. The GPO men laboured for the tradesmen.

Figure 19 – Little Tina Harvey on the Silver Birch site. Figure 20 – one pair of bungalows to wall height.

Figure 21 & 22 – Show that all trades had to work at the same time, bricklayers alongside carpenters and roofers. Each bungalow in each phase were competed in progression.

Chapter 8

And so, we build

It was a hard January waiting for news, while continuing to build the bungalows. As one might expect, the meetings of the scheme to discuss matters arising were less frequent in 1952, and were even less evident in 1953 due to the amount of building work that they all had to undertake. Those meetings that were held, were to discuss pressing matters: the build and changes, the hours being worked etc. A couple were held in the site hut - that was so large it could accommodate all the materials and equipment and the men - others were held in bungalows as they became available.

The build itself was hard graft and the commitment was exacting on everyone; all by now were working seventy hours a week plus travelling to and from the site. The lorry was an asset for many, as it could be used to drop off all those living to the south east of the city and its would make the route around regularly after each evenings work was done. Some, like Jimmy Thompson (the very fast bricklayer), had motorbikes and my father had a motorbike and sidecar. Reg used to cycle the distance because he could not take advantage of the lorry, as he lived to the west of the city. He used to cycle to work every day from Selly Oak and then cycle to the site after he had finished his shift at the G.P.O. This was followed by a hard few hours in the evenings, or a half day and a full day every Sunday. The eleven miles there and back was quite exhausting with all the manual labour that he would have to do, and even though he was a fit young man in his prime, the arduous travel and physical efforts began to take its toll. He recalls that on one Sunday, having finished the day at the site, he cycled homewards, and arriving in Bournville on that afternoon there was a cricket match on, so he stopped for a rest to observe the proceedings on the cricket square. Leaning his bike against the railings, he remained seated and within a short while he drifted off to sleep, still sitting on his bicycle. He woke up with a start: it was the early hours of the Monday morning, and by the time he got home it was 4am and he still had work that day.

He was becoming quite an expert on trench digging. They had spent those many hours practicing trench digging and wall building at Sandon Road under Harry's watch full gaze; each wall knocked down again, each trench filled in after every session. When the first trenches had been dug for 72 and 70 and the inspectors had conducted the pole dropping test, to measure how far the pole went into the ground to check that the footings for the foundations were correct, it was clear then that the G.P.O. trainees had learnt the task. Not an easy one when the site itself sloped substantially; hence the boggy parts where the water used to lay when the place was a large pond. Levelling the site to the architect's point meant in some cases digging quite far down; it was very noticeable at Reg and Dot's house (number 66). As a consequence, the foundations were much deeper to the rear than to the front on the property. According to Reg, when they dug they found that there were specific layers in the earth. The topsoil having been removed, there was a level of gravel and what Reg describes as 'a streak of black' beneath: a layer of ancient decomposed wood which was the remains of a forest, and laying on top of the solid bed of clay.

After trenches were dug to take the drain pipes, Jack Rogers and Ron Mason would lay the 5'x 4" pipes. It was then the time to mix the concrete for the foundations. Harry had always been very impressed with how meticulous everyone was in their attention to their tasks (that is evident by the quality of build that they undertook). As he remarked, it was 'a good build house even by today's standards.' That is high praise indeed from a man with such exacting standards and technical experience (with his own professional reputation to protect). He explained that there was no membrane in the platform, that they put shale in instead, so that all the water would drain away; they only had a couple of problems with this method in one or two of the houses which they rectified as they went on.

My mother and father used to tell me that my father had made an addition to our foundations at number 50; his bush hat and uniform from his time on active service in the Far East (Time Team might make an interesting find in 200 years or so). They also used to tell a story of my brother James (who was a toddling two in that year), falling from a plank bridging a freshly filled concrete trench. Suffice to say it did not end well when my mother realised. The women came on site when they could: it was nice to see the progress of their homes being created. As with other schemes, this was probably discouraged as the last thing that anyone needed in those long arduous months were any member of the team becoming distracted.

Ken describes them all as 'comrades in arms'; they had been thrown together by a necessity to build but they were not natural bed-fellows any of them: 'Like chalk and cheese'. Harry says that the trades were fairly autonomous, their own bosses, and got on with their jobs. The labourers, mainly the G.P.O., did most of the heavy manual work: clearing up, unloading, digging, mixing cement and mortar. They were able to accomplish some of the internal (non-visible) brickwork; the interior of the chimney for instance. As the trades were generally working for their employers during the day, and the G.P.O. shift pattern tended to be more accommodating to day work on the site, the trades would arrive at the scheme in the evening with the men from the G.P.O. having already spent that afternoon clearing and preparing the site for the incoming trades: moving bricks, timber, pipework, all to right locations in the correct quantities.

Reg had to keep juggling the morale of the 18 other members who had still not had confirmation regarding the issue of their licences. When he had been first aware by Solihull UDC back in the previous November that there was going to be a problem with the issue of the necessary licences (due to the suspension while Macmillan undertook his national survey), verbal reassurances were given by the Council that there was nothing to worry about, that the licences would come, and probably more promptly than they had been before.

At one stage, because of the critical lack of supply of licences, Solihull Council made a suggestion to the government that, as the majority of these schemes were Birmingham people (that their own Council had failed to make provision for), mobile licences might be made available from over the border. They qualified this further that, if this was not going to happen, then they wished all to make note that if Birmingham sought more land at some future date, it should be acknowledged that Solihull had taken much from the Birmingham overspill and that should be factored into any decisions made (the Boundaries Commission were at that time making plans to redraw the Birmingham boundary and a land-grab was feared by all of the surrounding areas adjacent to the city).

It is clear from the UDC minutes that their lobby to government for additional licences had paid dividends; the Ministry agreed not just to increase the available housing licenses as a whole to Solihull, but to more or less double them; this gave them considerable flexibility to begin to release batches of licences to all of the current schemes and those that seemed to be popping up everywhere. The next batch of 10 licences was approved for the four existing schemes (Silver Birch being one) on 6th February 1952, much to the relief of all on the scheme, not just the ten families that this would accommodate. It meant that of the four that were currently being erected, five more plots would have to be dug, levelled, trenches dug, drains laid, platforms made. There was going to be no rest and respite from what was now becoming a huge undertaking.

As everything was now at different stages in the scheme, with a few houses completed or near to completion, some in the stage of the build and others being laid out for foundations, it meant that the logistics of ordering materials and paying the invoices was becoming a complicated process. This is where having a financial officer as part of the scheme would set a model for good practice to other schemes. As had been agreed with the Bradford and Bingley Building Society, money would only be released as each of the stages were achieved: as a consequence, money came in tranches of funding. At the same time, materials and sub-contracting services were having to be ordered and paid for. Someone who understood double-entry book keeping was essential in order to maintain ordered financials and keep everything ticking over. My father would have had his work cut out for him at this point and going forward for some years to come; like all of his scheme comrades he had to continue his full-time job as a financial officer in a hospital; his work was relentless. As money came in, it was added to the cash balance; as orders were made and paid for, so too the deductions were all kept up to date. He was responsible for raising all of the purchase orders and making the approaches to the various suppliers. I remember all of these meticulously kept books and files that he retained until the day that he died.

After the problem with the ceramic roof tiles and the decision to contract out - based on the saving in time and manpower to the scheme - my father sought a contractor to do it. The remainder of the first batch of licences were duly tiled with the sand-faced, concrete tile as stipulated by the inspector from Solihull UDC. The whole process was very quick, as to be expected from dedicated tradesmen, but not without problems. It was when the scheme had progressed onto the footings and trenches for the next ten licences that the consequences of the tilers work became manifest. It was Harry and Reg that noticed; by that stage Reg had moved into number 66. The tiles began to shale and split and this cracking and flaking could be visibly seen from the roadside. Naturally, all were very annoyed. It was obvious that, in order to make the under-cut for profit margins, the tiling company had tried to get away with using a tile of very inferior quality. Knowing my father, he was probably particularly unimpressed. He could not abide poor workmanship; although having no skill, training or experience within construction, he had come from a family of master builders and stonemasons. He approached the firm with his complaint and argued with them that the job had to be rectified and the original quotation had to be adhered to, or they would be in breach of contract.

8. And so, we build

He got his way, although the tiling firm were probably unhappy at the prospect of more man-hours to do the same job, and they also had to replace the defective tiles at a cost to themselves. They were not that meticulous in the removal of those tiles, and just threw them from the roofs; they laid where they were thrown in many pieces (there are site photographs from the time shown all the tiles left and not cleared up by the tiling company). Suffice to say, for the rest of the build of the scheme they made sure the job was done properly first time.

As each family moved into their new home on a busy building site, they were issued with a rent book: 35/ per week was the rent to the Housing Association (the managing agents being Shipway and Doble). Ground rent was separate, at £13 per year payable to the landlord Mr Jack Cotton. The rent books clearly stipulated the regulations according to the Rent Act of 1938: no overcrowding, only the specified number in a dwelling, keeping the property and garden in good order, duty of care to other tenants. This was an important fact in all that would eventually follow. They were tenants of an association; they were building their own rented properties. None had any dreams or aspirations at that stage to be home-owners; they were just glad to get a roof over their heads, as many were in Solihull by taking advantage of self-help housing. What set a few apart like Silver Birch from the many associations in Solihull eventually, was the fact that they had brokered their own finance via a building society independently: a decision that was going to prove very worthwhile a little later into the story.

By now, the approaches to Solihull from other housing associations across the border in Birmingham had gone from a handful to many. There was only so much land available, but Solihull did know that there were two main advantages to encouraging, rather than discouraging, these willing men. Firstly, it gave a strong argument with the boundaries commission, should the need ever arise, for it to not re-determine boundaries in Birmingham's favour, as Solihull were helping their population to be housed. An important factor to remember was that Solihull was seeking a charter of incorporation to expand at the same time as all of these associations were building. The last thing the UDC needed was to lose land and that may lose the scale to justify that charter. The second advantage was due to how many of the associations were financed. As I have noted in the part one of this book, the 1936 Housing Act allowed for grant loans to be made at favourable interest rates, over a repayment period of 60 years. When an association made that contract with the authority, they became tenants of the authority; especially if the land was council-owned. Unlike those very few associations that had sought funding through independent means, those associations who went down the route of taking advantage of the loans via Solihull were, in effect, building council houses, and for an authority that still had targets to reach for the Ministry of Housing, it was win-win situation (it is important to note that all self-help houses were considered as council house licences, that is what made them so attractive).

In fact, it had begun to make a significant impact and as such, had come to the attention of the local MPs Martin Lyndsey (Solihull) and his Birmingham counterpart - Julius Silverman MP. To these men and others in government, it was proof-positive of the Conservative principles – that if a man is given a chance to make something of himself and his life that he will - and the complete antithesis to the welfare state, where all was taken care of. There was room now for those individuals with initiative, drive and determination to better themselves. For certain MPs, this message was not to be ignored, and in the case of the

8. And so, we build

MP for Solihull (whose Council had greater aspirations than to remain a UDC), a chance to promote the district for its far-thinking, egalitarian approach to housing not just its own population, but a considerable amount of prospective self-builders from Birmingham. It was enough for it to deserve a mention in the House of Commons with an invitation attached, to any member or minister who wished to observe for themselves this undertaking, as Martin Lyndsey MP concluded in his speech for February 29th 1952 with his reference to the upcoming coronation:

> "These are the men with guts and enterprise, who are getting on with the job instead of waiting for something to be done for them. Often, they work a 78 - hour week, whilst being paid for working 44 hours. I like to think that they are typical of what we hope are going to be the new Elizabethans."
> (Hansard)

In support of his 'plea' that the government should offer all assistance possible to these schemes, Julius Silverman MP (Erdington, Birmingham) replied that it was Birmingham people that had gone to Solihull to build, and he cited the following case of a factory-supported scheme:

> "The hon. Member referred particularly to one scheme in his constituency, that is, the Fortitude Housing Association connected with the Dunlop factory. There are 50 men involved, and the lastex section of Dunlop has given them every assistance in developing their training. Some of them, of course, were building workers before they went into the factory. They have contributed something like 12 houses up to the present. It is very obvious that schemes like this can make a valuable contribution to the housing problem in places like the Birmingham area."

But he stressed that the self-help movement was likely to be hindered by a now familiar problem:

> "In Birmingham, we have a housing waiting list of about 60,000 and people who are coming into the city far outnumber the number of houses which are being built by the Local Authority. The bottleneck in Birmingham is not so much building material as shortage of building labour. The consequence is that these people are building in the Birmingham area houses which would otherwise not have been built. That is the important point to remember."

Materials and union dissatisfaction were likely to cause great difficulties for those trying to help themselves: indeed, both of these problems were encountered by Silver Birch scheme. My father, Joe – having responsibility for purchase orders – had the experience of some suppliers who were refusing to assist housing associations for fear of repercussions from the professional trades and contractors. There was some hiatus within the industry that, because everyone was seeking the same sources of supply for the same materials and items such as bathroom fitments and various plumbing supplies, the trades should take priority whenever there were shortages. Additionally, it may have been perceived that the housing associations, by virtue of the fact that they were building for themselves, were taking work and, by that

8. And so, we build

fact, income away from professionally-hired contractors. Suppliers knew that they would depend on the valuable custom of their tradesmen eventually, and were desperate to keep their loyalty. It was certainly a virtue of the scheme that so many professional tradesmen were building on Silver Birch, as that did help with managing to purchase a job-lot of sanitation ware for the scheme, for instance, as long as it was bought upfront in bulk. Ken tells of the powers of Sam Marfleet - a carpenter who lived at number 56 - who could manage to get deals to get most things, even when they were extremely scare, such as draining boards.

It was at that time that the association had decided to make all of the houses standard in fitting. The realisation came that to purchase in quantity would invariably be cheaper, and that there were too many possible outcomes and indecisions that could come if everyone was allowed umpteen options over fitments and fittings, so it made more sense to standardise all. Certain changes had to be made to the final bungalow design, either due to an existing anomaly in the architect's plans, or a ruling by Solihull UDC planning. The architects had incorrectly drawn the plans and had the chimney passing through the ridge: as a consequence, a change had to be made in the kitchen area where the coke fire was sited. This led to an arrangement of a double alcove in order to provide a supporting structure for the chimney, which now had a straight flue rather than a bent one. This alcove became adapted for different things: in my parents' house, ours contained our very large gas boiler and the other our standing fridge/freezer; no doubt many interesting modifications and integrated units have utilised in more recent times.

The second modification was the position of the kitchen. All the women - including my mother - loved the idea of the kitchen being sited at the rear of the house, so that they would be able to look out onto the garden and watch their children whilst enjoying the view. Unfortunately, it meant that the third bedroom would face a neighbour's third bedroom (this was the time before large fences were installed, or large hedges grew). The Council would not approve this, so the women had to sacrifice their dream for a kitchen-facing a yard. Many ended up with veranda arrangements that abutted the eventual garages that were built. My parents left theirs as a yard with trees and shrubs; at least my mother was still able to watch the birds while she cooked. The third bedroom in many cases became a dining room years later, when dormer roofs were added to accommodate extra bedrooms on a second storey.

It may have been as a consequence of a national heightening of awareness of the acute housing-shortage that interest was raised all of a sudden with other curious people. Dot talks about coach loads arriving every Sunday to look around to see what all these self-builders were doing. Some were coming because they had a desire to do the same and wanted to see how it was done; others because they just wanted a day out and to be a bit nosey. Of course, as Dot recalls, you could not be rude and turn them away, and they always wanted to look around the interiors. Dot was always obliging no matter how difficult it was for her, and it was difficult. Not only did she have her little girl Tina to look after, but part of the standardisation of the bungalows was the laying of brown Semastic floor tiles (most covered with carpets as soon as that became affordable). The problem with these tiles, as I remember, was that they marked very easily, which led to having to be constantly cleaned.

As you might imagine, a muddy site with no pavements, on a rainy Sunday afternoon, and a busy young housewife's timetable do not quite mix. These 'incomers' would process in packs in and out of Dot's house and by the end of the afternoon, not only was she exhausted but she had a cleaning job of monumental proportions to do. Added to that, if Dot

8. And so, we build

had been particularly accommodating that Sunday lunchtime, many of the men from the site would have taken advantage of her kind offer for Sunday lunch, and she would have obliged with excellent hospitality.

It was a great problem for the young mothers living on a building site. They had prams to manoeuvre through mud and over planks of wood to get to the concrete road. There were no footpaths at that time and not for some time to come. Although they had got their house, they now had very little money to do anything to make it homelier other than with what they had brought with them, or that they could make for themselves. Dreams of beautiful gardens would have to stay as dreams, at least until the topsoil was levelled and then for some time to come. But they did have that much-needed house and to all of them the amount of space that they had was marvellous; a few more years of minor discomfort was a small sacrifice for all that they had been rewarded with.

The work-life balance was beginning to pose a problem for some in early 1952. The realisation that the overtime at work had to be forgone in order to remain committed to the scheme, was a very complicated problem for a few members: paid overtime meant more money to live and possibly save for extras later. It is recorded in the minutes of the association from April 1952 that this had become a serious enough issue to have to insist on a revision for how hours worked on the scheme had to be accounted for. Up to this point, it had been a reasonably flexible arrangement: the commitment was for 20 hours in any week. However, some would do more some weeks and less on others. The problem was that a few were now not making up their lost hours, leaving the rest of the scheme having to undertake extra work. Harry insisted that hours would have to be accounted for weekly, and that in future those that failed to undertake their individual commitment had to explain to Harry (as foreman) their reasons, and when they intended to fulfil their obligations.

Silver Birch was run like a tight ship; it had to be. Those that had finished might well have been less enthusiastic to continue as they were able to move in, but that notion of comradeship prevailed, for if it had not been for all those who were still building (and in some cases still waiting for their licenses) no one would have been able to move in at all. The impetus of the 'team effort' continued unabated. Whether they were now onsite and making a much longer commute to their place of work every day or not, they kept up the same momentum from start to finish, no matter how fatigued they were all beginning to feel, no matter how the hours, days, weeks and months of effort now seemed relentless. They must finish the job for everyone - after all, the faster they finished, the sooner they could enjoy the fruits of their arduous labours.

Figure 23 & 24 – Health and Safety? Observe the height of the scaffolding, the lack of hard-hats and safety boots.

Figures 25 & 26 – *The muddy building site, it would be a while before gardens could be afforded. The pile of tiles thrown down and left by the roofers who had to return to replace their poor-quality tiles*

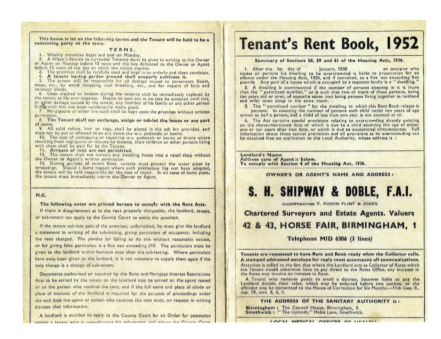

Figure 27 – The rent book – all the owners/builders rented their houses from their association.
Figure 28 – Ebrington Avenue today 48 & 46

Chapter 9

Topping Out

The arduous toil continued without a let up. In July 1952, the final eight licences were released. The Silver Birch Association still had a long way to go before they could see a finishing line. All members were now accounting for their hours on a weekly basis, and this meant that any needs for overtime at their places of work had to be restricted. The endless round of digging of trenches and the laying of drains continued, as did the Council's continual need to inspect all; to everyone this routine became the norm.

The health and safety left something to be desired by today's exacting standard. It was just not an issue then; had it been, I doubt any of the schemes would have be able to build in the first place. Scaffolding was erected that did not have guard rails, hand-tools were used above head-height. Safety clothing was not even considered; it was as much as each member could do to find an old pair of work boots and old trousers; hard hats and eye protection were a complete nonsense at that time. However, there were very few incidents of note, again a mark of the times. Pat Rowson recalls that Oscar was below some of the bricklayers working at height, when a brick fell and gashed his head:

"He needed three stiches!"

Notwithstanding all of this and the many lacking any previous experience, the close governance of Harry (and the professional experience of the other tradesmen) must have been at the root of why so few accidents ever occurred.

Despite four schemes all building in close proximity; all having used the same architect, all being Birmingham people who had migrated to Solihull in order to take advantage of the available land, none seemed to fraternise or mix. According to Reg, Harry and Ken, they were simply just too busy working on the scheme to have the time to pay much attention to what the others were doing. However, they were aware that the other schemes around them were not making similar progress or indeed seemed as well organised. The good fortune or common sense of the idea that Reg had to encourage trades to team up with G.P.O. in order to build the houses, appears to have been the determining factor that enabled this scheme to shoot ahead of its neighbours. In fact, they advanced at a much quicker rate than the other G.P.O. scheme initiated by George Lavender in Tallington Road in Sheldon. These other schemes simply lacked the skill and expertise to be able to keep the same pace of build going. There are reports that the Tallington Road scheme only had one skilled bricklayer; for a scheme of 50 bungalows over two sites, this was quite a challenge.

Of the three other schemes, adjacent to Silver Birch; U Build It, Tyburn and Sparkhill, all three needed to employ a raft of sub-contractors. That in itself created massive delays, as the acute shortages within the industry of manpower still persisted: if the same pool of skilled men were being requested, lead-in times and waiting times for the completion of jobs increased. Added to that, despite the financial support that these schemes could access

9. Topping out

through their firms, they were still like the men on the Silver Birch scheme: on relatively modest schemes trying to make ends meet. Every sub-contractor that had to be paid for meant that more money had to be found, which would often add to the waiting time as the money simply was not there.

Silver Birch had the skills that had been recommended by the man from the Ministry in that phone call that Reg had made two years previously: there was very little that the scheme lacked. Where there had been an obvious need (such as for the tiling of the roofs), a contractor was employed (and now making sure that the tiles were of good quality and at the originally agreed price). Generally, any additional needs of skill could be accommodated by the team. Mr Thorp was a good mechanic and took care of the good old faithful G.P.O. lorry. Horace Plume was a jobbing builder (jack-of-all-trades) and could turn his hand to most things that were required. As I have already mentioned, Sam Marfleet was excellent at finding sources of things that were in extremely short supply. Each of the lead-hands on any of the trades; electrics, plumbing, had someone assigned as an assistant. For instance: Jack Rogers was assisted by Ron Mason for drains; Sid Steadman as plumber was assisted by Ken Robotham; and Harry Foster as the main electrician was assisted by Dan Ready (the man who had cycled a long way in the snow to beg a place on the scheme or his girlfriend would refuse to marry him).

The excellent relationships that my father developed with the suppliers owed as much to his personal charm as his prompt payment; 'neither a borrower or a lender be' as he always insisted. The lorry driver who used to deliver the bricks for the scheme appreciated the men from the G.P.O. simply because there was always someone on site to unload promptly, which meant the driver could return and collect another consignment for elsewhere; two jobs in one day was more money for the driver. Many people were supportive and admired the self-builders for their grit and determination, hence the frequent visits to the site just to see how it could be accomplished. As Ken remarks, they did not have time to reflect or think, or even to consider how they were operating:

> "The will of the association, formed without us knowing. They were all extremely focussed. They needed to be to get the job done."

As much as the G.P.O. men admired the trades for their skills and abilities, Ken feels that this admiration was mutual, and that the trades admired the grit of what may have previously been perceived as 'soft' men to apply themselves to the task.

Whatever professional admiration and respect that was shared during those times of building were not the foundations of any prolonged social interaction. These two distinctly different groups came together for a moment, for a process driven out of necessity. After it was all done they would separate once more into their social networks and have very little to do with one another. Any future social interaction tended to be driven by the women who would endeavour to keep things going. It helped that most of the G.P.O. women had been recruited around about the same time, so by that fact were the same age. Dot explains that Dennis Foster's wife Rita had been her boss at work, and that Cath Moseley had been her bridesmaid; there was a social circle there, which expanded a little after the build, as the other housewives interacted with each other and the lives of their growing offspring.

Reg considers the relationship of all of the men as having been 'social not really socialising'; there was that overriding need to accomplish a task and that was all. There were only fleeting moments of distraction such as the time Reg recalls throwing a snowball at Ken

9. Topping out

Robotham who was a big man, and Reg was upended in the snow. There was no time to be jolly and play practical jokes, unlike the prevailing work culture known to all of someone sending a young, green, apprentice for a long-stand, or a short weight, sky-hooks, left-handed spanners, elbow grease, the list is never ending. Or the poor unsuspecting young G.P.O. messenger boys being sent on a fool's errand for a fog lamp. There was just not the time available for tomfoolery. However, my brother James recalls being aware of beautiful singing drifting across the road to his very young ears, as he stood in what would be our garden, when Horace and Jo Plume's bungalow was being plastered by the Irish sub-contractor: by all accounts he had a stunning singing voice; though it was a rare occasion that he was actually sober on site. There were some nicknames given to our worthy team; Reg Smith was known as Baldy, for the obvious reason that he had no hair, Dennis Foster was never referred to as Dennis, but always as Dickie, and Jeoff Walker - who had a reputation for betting on the horses - was known as Jasper. Our own neighbour Bill Sternberg was known as Dutchy. The story goes that as he had a Dutch name (although he knew of no Dutch relatives). He was asked to join the Dutch navy during the war, and afterwards the nickname stuck. Reg himself was christened by Noreen Walker as 'our instigator' and that stuck too.

What was the everyday picture of life for those that moved in gradually, besides the lack of footpaths and the mud; what sort of amenities did this area offer young families? At the end of the avenue, just around the corner on Lode Lane (to become Old Lode Lane) is Hatchford Brook Junior School, which each one of us attended in turn. There was a row of shops immediately adjacent to the avenue - the local shops of the type where every shopkeeper knew each resident by name. We were very well appointed for shops, having: a grocer, a green-grocer, a fish monger, a butcher, a newsagent, a tobacconist, and, to the delight of us smaller inhabitants, two sweet shops within spitting distance of the end of our road, and joy of joys - Jarrett's Toy shop (many hours were spent staring at the delights in the window with hopeful expectation).

Hobs Moat was just under development and it would be a while before the vast parade of shops there would be available. There were other shops though, if you turned right out of Ebrington Avenue and walked towards Elmdon Park (adjacent to Land Rover and Elmdon Airport - now Birmingham International Airport). In that parade at Hatchford Brook was a fish and chip shop and a café; indeed, we were very well provided for. I still remember Phil the Co-op milkman with his electric milk float, who would let you ride on it with him just while he delivered in the avenue, and there was a bread-man who delivered too. My brother recalls in his day there were two competing bread deliveries, and the coal man.

It was still a very rural location when the bungalows were first built. This was long before the Birmingham urbanisation would swallow Coventry Road and Sheaf Lane at Sheldon, and it would go from a tree-lined boulevard of service roads to the six-lane junction with over-head traffic lights that it has now become. If you walked a little way down Lode Lane from Ebrington Avenue towards the Wheatsheaf Public House on the corner of Coventry Road, there used to be a small farm, near where Mahoney's is now (then, Mahoney's was called Martins). Small children would be taken down to see the animals and feed them, as Ken remembers fondly doing with his son. My brother recalls he and the Ebrington Avenue gang scrumping under-ripe fruit and all suffering belly ache as a consequence. And there was a 'gang' by all accounts in my brother's day. Dot remarks that most of the girls were born at her end of the avenue (she must have had a monopoly having

9. Topping out

three daughters); at the other end of the avenue, there were 22 boys born. Of course, this had consequences; two football teams, gangs of stone-throwing young boys and all that goes with that. By the time I came along, all were grown and gone: most families were settling down to emptier nests and the avenue no longer rang with the shouts of gaggles of boys.

By January 1953, Harry was able to advise the concerned members of the association that holidays could be booked by the end of the following July. The pressure was on everyone to get the job done as soon as possible: all those who had finished and moved in still had their commitment to the others waiting to finish the building. Obviously, with more bungalows finished than there were waiting to be built, it now meant that more man-power could be devoted to those last few. It did have consequences to those already in their homes: any DIY or gardening had to take a back seat, not that there was much surplus income to lay out on other things. Horace Plume, Sid Steadman and Ken Quiney were all single men at the time of the ballot and right at the end of the queue, but Ken recalls that it only took one month to build his bungalow: the very last. It was a great example of their democracy in action that, despite being the chairman of the scheme and having married Pauline in 1952, they were the last to move in, and they loved their new home.

Like all of the wives on the scheme, Pauline was so proud of what they had achieved, and it is not to be forgotten that it was a joint effort for husband and wife. The men may have undertaken the physical work on site, and put many hours into the building of the bungalows with all the associated travelling, but the women had to do much on their own to look after the children that were being born and, in Dot's case, additional administration work as well to support the scheme. Joan Pestridge commented that it was two years of their lives, but that is was so well worth it in the end: all of space and the lovely environment was so much more than any had dreamed of. No longer having to live cheek-by-jowl with relatives in cramped conditions was an absolute blessing. Every member of the scheme was soon hosting visits from envious relatives who admired their hard work and devotion for such a lovely outcome.

Beryl Rose was in the same position as most: a young mother on a limited income. Norman and Beryl found it very hard for a number of years trying to make ends meet, and unfortunately Norman died at a relatively young age, leaving Beryl very little alternative but to move away. Ken and Marge Foster also found the struggle too much and eventually sold up and moved away. However, it is a mark of the scheme and how much their hard work and efforts meant to each of them, that the vast majority remained. In the beginning, they were tenants of the Silver Birch Housing Association and glad to have a roof over their heads, but all that was set to change.

By the time the last bungalows were finished, the euphoria amongst the members was very high, as is evident in the minutes of the AGM in July 1953. Among many things discussed were the accounts, and following, the disposal of tools and equipment from the scheme, and my father proposed that they might invite Councillor Maurice Mell to come and open the last bungalow. At that moment, the idea of a formal opening was enthusiastically greeted and it was decided unanimously to do this; they formed a sub-committee to arrange it all. It is also marked in the minutes for Solihull UDC that following September that this first scheme was due to finish and that an official opening may be in order. However, the fatigue that had accumulated following twenty-eight months of very hard work began to take it's affect as the adrenaline fell away: everyone just felt too tired and desperately needed a break and so the opening never happened.

The final meetings of that summer were to resolve all outstanding debts and commitments, and realise any additional income made through the sale of the plant and equipment. In those minutes, as far back as August 1953, a discussion was starting as regards self-ownership. It was becoming obvious to some that they were one step away from being home owners rather than Council tenants by default. We often equate the 'Right-to-buy' principle with a strategy adopted under Margaret Thatcher's government, but as they say, there is nothing new under the sun: much of what the present government has done towards the housing situation, and their predecessors in the coalition and before, is neither visionary or new. Much can have its lineage traced directly back to those strategies implemented by Herbert Macmillan back in the early 1950's.

The Conservative government had set itself an enormous task in order to win that crucial 1951 election, a task that they had watched their Labour colleagues fail to do directly after the war. As Attlee had declared that he was to build a million homes over the term of his government, Churchill insisted that the Conservatives would build three-hundred thousand a year. Martin Lindsay had brought everyone's attention to the plight of the self-helpers in Solihull: these hard-working, dedicated men prepared to get themselves stuck-in, in order that their families were housed. It was becoming apparent to those in government that, if an additional incentive were given - that of home ownership as an end result - it may well encourage more to take the plunge and make that commitment to self-build. Any strategy that might help to achieve this high target for house building had to be encouraged, and offering those who had engaged in such a gargantuan effort to have the right to buy their home seemed the logical next step.

The concept to buy is mentioned several times in 1953 in the Silver Birch Association minutes, however, there was so much more to resolve and monies to return to members that this idea, on the back of enormous fatigue, was merely a consideration at that stage. Never the less, it did influence any initial considerations for taking over the management from the agents, as there were so many that were keen on ownership. They would have to play a waiting game with the rest.

It had always been envisaged that, after everything had been sold and all the debts met, there may well be some money to be returned to the members from their original deposits. My father was tasked with disposing of the faithful G.P.O. lorry: this he did well, as it made more from that sale than it had cost them to buy. By early October, the association was able to return the princely sum of £25 5/ 6d to each of the members; having made a capital deposit each of £45 back in 1950, this was not a bad return. Another issue concerned with only being tenants had become apparent by that meeting: the laying of the footpaths. Mothers were still struggling with toddlers, prams and shopping to get to the hard surface of the road. It was explained to the members that this was up to the freeholder to resolve, who had insisted that, until all of the members' boundary walls had been built, very little could be done.

Three years were to pass before serious action would begin to move all of the association members to their eventual home-owning aspirations. In those Annual General Meetings in between, again the footpaths were becoming a point of contention, as the landlord was insisting on the members raising the level; likewise, the members were resisting and leaving it to the landlord to resolve. Over those years, enquiries were made as to what costs may be incurred if they were to buy their houses as individuals. One of those additional costs to be factored-in was the subsidy that had been granted by the exchequer, subsequently, passed on by the local Council. All was calculated and surprisingly the expenses involved appeared to be only slightly more than current rents that were being re-paid. This was not by any means prohibitive for most, but for some probably with their already over-stretched budgets (and any personal objections to the concept of home-owning) just too much at the wrong moment.

By the end of 1956, the tide was turning in the favour of those who wished to buy. This was certainly helped by careful management of any re-payment due to Solihull UDC of the subsidy, and the fact that mortgages had been initially over-calculated had not allowed for those members who had already built garages on stand-alone mortgages. After some serious negotiations amongst neighbours and members by January 1957, all had agreed to pass Evershed and Tompkinson's motion to allow the trustees to act on behalf of the scheme to facilitate each member to purchase his own house. The block mortgage to Bradford and Bingley Building Society was to be redeemed, and a new individual mortgage of $1/28^{th}$ would be issued to each member: once all had been agreed, it was found that these mortgages were very favourable indeed. Years later, the association would make that final leap into the unknown and purchase their freehold; a move that would finally prove that old adage; 'an Englishman's home is his castle'.

This is the story of a marvellous group of people who worked through adversity to build their own homes when there was absolutely no chance of ever living in any home other than that to be shared with others. All of the hardships that they had to endure over that initial period of three years, to enable them to live under their own roof, had given them the dream that they all desired: becoming the rightful owner of that piece of their history was an expectation none had ever believed possible. This was not an easy road for any of them, husbands or wives; to build 28 bungalows in 28 months with limited skills and working in full-time employment was an amazing achievement. Harry was a man of exacting standards; he had to be, to be foreman and clerk of works of so many fleet projects. Anything he did in his own time also reflected on him, as such he was a hard man to please, however, he stood firm in his opinion that they were one of the best built houses that he ever worked on, the quality of each build was exceptional.

The question as to whether it could be done today was posed by my brother to each of the surviving interviewees. All agreed it would be an impossible task in today's climate, and probably best summed up in the words of Ken:

> "There are people that self-build… but not the way that we did it… we been brought up in a different sort of environment… to start with they haven't had the discipline of the war, and the urgency that came with it… You had to look after yourself!... Nowadays, everybody expects to be looked after… I can't imagine ever getting twenty-eight men to build twenty-bungalows… It was a case of necessity and discipline."

The three main characteristic traits that set these individuals apart from many are simple to identify: determined - not one man lacked that same determination both as individuals and as a team; willing to make sacrifice and endure hardship; disciplined - it was the discipline of a generation that had been honed by war. I suppose after a war, after active service for some,

9. Topping out

this may not have seemed like much of a hardship or a sacrifice, but in my opinion, these three traits were necessary pre-requisites to make it all happen.

I grew up in the avenue some years after my elder siblings (they being of that generation when 22 boys dominated one end of the avenue providing 2 football teams). I didn't really become aware of what it all meant until I made my annual trek up and down the avenue for my mother delivering her Christmas cards from when I was about eight (she was house-bound by then). All these people (I hardly knew any of them, just by their formal titles on their envelopes) would enquire after my parents, occasionally a comment of admiration for my father, which I would find rather odd. I didn't really appreciate the momentous occasion when the freehold was purchased, apart from my mother insisting to me how important it was to own your own land. By that time, any 'comradeship' that Ken described had fragmented: G.P.O. mixed with G.P.O., trades mixed with trades. My dad was the oddball, being neither 'fish nor fowl'; we ended up hidden behind our four enormous silver birch trees, our garden wall, and high privet hedges. For a very brief time in all of their lives, roles had been reversed: bosses had become labourers and everyone had admired everyone else, to enable the undertaking of a lifetime.

In the next chapter, I am going to quote re-tell some tales from other self-build schemes in Solihull that remain in unpublished material in Solihull Central Library, to compare experiences and achievements. I will endeavour to explain how and why Solihull finished their adventures in self-help. For now, I honour all those members of Silver Birch that finished ahead of all others and broke the ground for several hundreds of schemes nationally:

72	Harry and Joan Pestridge	Foreman	1st license
70	Ken and Margie Robotham	Plumber	2nd license
68	Jimmy and Jean Clayton	Labourer*^	3rd license
67	Sid and Beryl Steadman	Plumber	
66	Reg and Dot Harvey	Labourer*	4th license
65	Horace and Jo Plume	Various	
64	Reg and Joan Smith	Bricklayer	5th license
63	Jack and Dot Rogers	Labourer*^^	
62	Charlie and Ivy Josebury	Bricklayer	6th license
61	Ken and Pauline Quiney	Labourer*	
60	Arthur and Lil Crutchley	Bricklayer	7th license
59	Harry and Dorothy Foster	Electrician	
58	Bob and Rene Roberts	Labourer*	8th license
57	Dan and Marion Ready	Electrician	
56	Sam and Avis Marfleet	Labourer*	9th license
55	Jeoff and Noreen Walker	Labourer*	
54	Bill and Dot Morgan	Labourer*	10th license
53	Oscar and Pat Rowson	Labourer*	
52	Reg and Ann Thorp	Mechanic	
51	Jim and Norma Thompson	Bricklayer	
50	Joe and Margaret Debney	Labourer	
49	Denis and Rita Foster	Labourer*	

9. Topping out

48	Bill and Sheila Sterenberg	Labourer*	
46	Norman and Beryl Rose	Carpenter	
44	Ken and Marge Foster	Labourer	
42	George and Edna Spittle	Bricklayer	
40	Ron and Betty Mason	Labourer*	
38	Charlie and Cath Moseley	Labourer*	

*these were all the men from the G.P.O. ^Jimmy Clayton was also a carpenter.
^^Jack Rogers was an engineer for the G.P.O.- hence, expert for drains.

Figure 29 – Dot and Reg Harvey

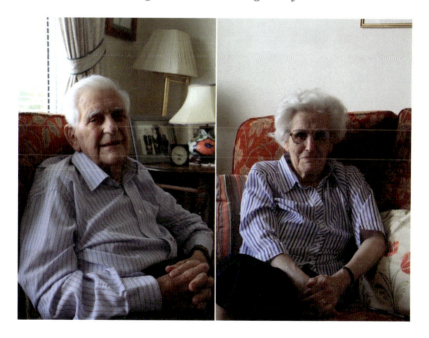

Figure 30 – Harry and Joan Pestridge

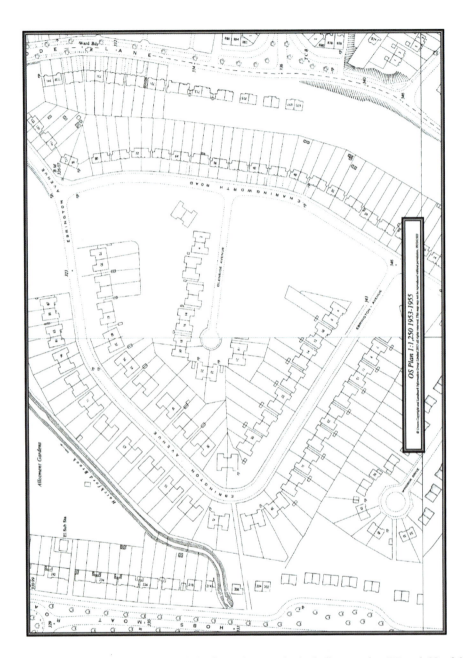

Figure 31 – Showing numbers 72 – 38 and the five pairs opposite including number 55 and 63 of the Silver Birch Scheme (Note – the floorplan of Silver Birch is distinctively different to the other scheme).
"With grateful thanks to www.old-maps.co.uk and Ordnance Survey for allowing me to reproduce this image."

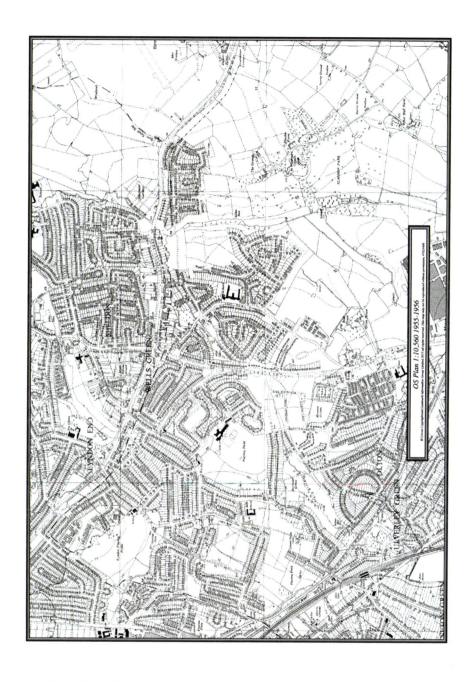

Figure 32 – *Shows the rapid development of the area that took place in six years.*
"*With grateful thanks to www.old-maps.co.uk and Ordnance Survey for allowing me to reproduce this image.*"

Chapter 10

All in the scheme of things

Of course, Silver Birch is only part of the story, which was a much bigger tale both locally and nationally. There is no doubt that the first schemes were those that were nurtured in Birmingham and bore the great fruit with the help of the aspirations of Solihull UDC. In this chapter, I am going to project the time-line of events that occurred in that dynamic decade of the 1950's by using the minutes of Solihull UDC and their Housing Committee, along with three unpublished stories of self-help schemes that were in the same predicament that the families from Silver Birch were. Their tales not only enhance the telling of this story, but the narrative left emphasises the differences between schemes that were well-catered for with access to skills, and those that were not. The skills gap and lack of essential knowledge (that had been stressed as required by the 'man from the Ministry' in the phone call in 1950) caused huge delays in time and led to financial problems for those that were ill-equipped; it also led to the demise of an organisation established to assist the self-helpers.

In addition to these two sources of evidence, I have included exerts and quotation from local newspapers of the time. This is to illustrate how the movement was hailed as a success in these complex times for Solihull, but equally was under threat from the backlash that would inevitably follow the mass-building of council houses that had gone on within the district. Once the establishment of the borough was assured (and the removal of national financial incentive), this would eventually no longer be necessary to support the expansion of Solihull.

As I have implied in chapter 2, not just Solihull but the urban centres of The Midlands had suffered considerably from bomb-damage and a lack of investment in the infrastructure for the whole duration of the war. It is hard to visualise these days, when there is no longer a British car manufacturing industry, how essential that industry was, not just to those companies but to the gross domestic product of the country as a whole. Nearly all the large car manufactures were centred in or around Birmingham and Coventry: they manufactured all of the cars for the national and (many) for the international market and depended on a huge network of suppliers and services, again locally. During the war, each firm had played an essential part in munition and aircraft production, hence the strategic targeting of the Luftwaffe with devastating consequences. To have a car factory in your local area could promote enormous inward investment and assist in that local rebuilding and regeneration post war.

This is to some extent why Solihull UDC made great efforts to find various solutions to the housing of the employers from the Rover Company: if that company could be allowed to develop and flourish, it could only bring a considerable amount of economic regeneration that was critical to Solihull as a whole. The infrastructure of the district was unsustainable. Much of what had been started during the interwar years lay abandoned, roads unadopted, housing estates unfinished or never started, street lighting and essential services were in a mess and Solihull had very little money to make any improvements. A headline from the Warwickshire County News dated 28.4.45 illustrates the frustrations of local residents to what was perceived as a failing Council. It reads: 'Sheldon residents do not resent the rate increase but they do want the Council to take over the roads.' It appears at that time that, like Ebrington Avenue, many roads had been laid in that area by prospective housing developers pre-war; now with the shortages in materials and manpower (and these things being so desperately needed everywhere else and no longer being available), these schemes had stopped. Further, the housing contractors were in the position of strength knowing that they were so vital to the general recovery of the whole area and, as such, they would no longer offer their services at those costs originally agreed seven years previously. Solihull had no choice but to make a rate increase to all householders in an effort to raise the income to address the problems. This quotation highlights the Council's response, which was just as frustrating to them:

> "Replying. Councillor Freeman said that the Council would be only too glad to secure adoption, but developers of estates in Sheldon had either not completed the roads or had not built them to the standards required. The developers were in a strong position now. The agreement to relieve house purchasers of road charges had not, in many cases specifies any dates by which the roads were now to be completed, and now the developer could plead lack of labour and material with justification. The Council was not all powerful. He himself when first elected, was surprised how many ways the Council was hedged about laws, rules and restrictions."

The prospect of losing such a vital employer as the Rover Company to another town or site, was not one that the Council would have welcomed. Consequently, all avenues, including the formation of housing associations, were explored, which of course enabled Solihull to appreciate the value of housing associations to their plans. It is probably because of this fact, combined with the general lack of land in Birmingham on which to build, that other companies, such as Joseph Lucas and Dunlop began to set their sights on the housing of their employees within the confines of Solihull.

Both companies had groups of employees' approach Solihull as early as 1950, having formed company-sponsored schemes, with the intention of securing a site. It is supposed that George Lavender's experimental self-build of a bungalow within close proximity had been completed. He had proved it could be done and had formed the G.P.O. Fordrough Lane scheme and they were in the process of gaining planning permission for their site in Tallington Road in Sheldon. This venture may well have been influential as to the area then chosen by those firms seeking land adjacent to Lode Lane in Sheldon, or could be the land that was ear-marked by the Council as that which needed development and investment, as it had been abandoned by the pre-war house developers.

Solihull had managed to deliver the house building targets that had been set for the region over the term of the Attlee government. It has to be said that not suffering from significant bomb damage meant that land did not have to be made safe and cleared first, and this cut costs and was less time-consuming. Once the change of government occurred in 1951 to the same political persuasion as the Council, it was even more imperative that Solihull was seen to be supporting the party strategy to increase house building. Additionally, the fear of

10. All in the scheme of things

boundaries under threat and land being taken for Birmingham's needs was palpable. The more Birmingham people that could be helped to be housed by Solihull UDC, the greater support they may have to not only protect their existing borders, but look to a possible future of expansion. It is minuted in May 1950 that Solihull was actively seeking a Charter of Incorporation as a borough.

What is also evident from the Council minutes is that the employees of Joseph Lucas Ltd (who would eventually build in Ebrington Avenue) had approached Solihull UDC as early as June 1950, and that the workers of Dunlop Rubber Company had followed by September. Both of these employer-backed schemes had considerable financial and material advantage above those schemes that had been initiated by the G.P.O. As I have explained, as civil servants the G.P.O. were unable to receive any financial assistance; in the case of private employees it was at the discretion of the employer. Both firms had a need to keep a stable and secure workforce: uncertainty and displacement was not conducive to good productivity. It is certain that in most incidences of the self-help schemes, it required one individual man to become inspired to action and encourage others, rather than any employers or outside agencies driving the process. It would have been self-defeating to try to encourage the formation of a group to undertake such an enormous project of self-sacrifice; all of the prospective builders would have to be keen or the whole project would fail. It is wise to assume that in each case, including the company-supported schemes, there would have been a protagonist (as Norma Walker referred to Reg Harvey as "our instigator", or as is the case with Fordrough Lane G.P.O., George Lavender – "the great white chief"). That is not to say that with some schemes it did take more external encouragement than for others. This is probably why the government in 1936 foresaw the need to support any external, umbrella agency that may form, as this could be beneficial to concepts' success, hence the hint of financial support for such agencies in the 1936 Housing Act. As self-build was to rise over the next 24 months from 1951, this possibility of funding for 'guidance' would feature in the thinking certainly of George Lavender, and in the thinking of others with self-interest, to the former's detriment.

Interestingly, it is Dunlop Rubber Company that appears to have organised faster than Joseph Lucas Ltd. As the minutes of September 1950 from the housing committee discuss, this newly formed housing association, now named Fortitude, was seeking land in Ebrington Avenue (they built elsewhere). It is possible that the Council were still taking tentative steps and beginning to explore how it all could be done, and as we know Silver Birch, Lucas (to become U Build It), Tyburn and Sparkbrook were close on their heels. Fortitude were also in discussions with Birmingham, which may have delayed their start while they considered all options. However, by December 1950, all five associations are minuted that the Council were considering the benefits of obtaining additional licences by encouraging self-help. It is also minuted in the same part that a central organisation was being formed; this would Mr George Lavender, who was being seen as the man with the knowledge of how to do things, having built the bungalow already within the district and having established the first scheme. It was in the interest (as he had left his previous employment and was now full-time in his advisory role) of this central organisation to have involvement with all of these five infant schemes. Four schemes took advantage of membership (loosely); Silver Birch preferred to keep its own autonomy. Planning assent came through for all five schemes within weeks of one another; Fortitude gaining permission the beginning of April for a development of 30 houses on Lode Lane (that would change) and the other four schemes were approved at the end of April.

Rex Grogan, a member of the Fortitude scheme, wrote an account in 2009 called "'We built with Fortitude' Recollections of a self-help housing association". From this text, it is clear that the first houses built by Fortitude (Dunlop) were two on Lode Lane (now Old Lode Lane). After completing these two houses, which were then opened, they went on to build more houses on this site and were then given another site in Fallowfield Road.

Rex's book is witty and charming, full of anecdotes and images; it is a shame that it has not had a wider readership. Rex notes from the start the feelings of frustration felt by most when the massive austerity and struggle continued unabated post-war. He quotes the often-said phrase 'we really did win, didn't we?' In his jovial fashion, he describes the problems of trying to get a council house in Birmingham:

"…Council house Allocation.

'Eight children? Certainly sir/madam you can have the next being built. Just married? Forget it for at least 10 years. What are in-laws for? Waiting to get married? You'd be lucky."

He talks about Arthur Hill, seen as the originator of the idea for Dunlop, having learned about the G.P.O. and George Lavender. He was quite impressed with the support from Solihull, who he had previously considered quite 'stuffy' and he did not think that they would be quite as encouraging as they were. He does further qualify that, 50 years on, he felt 'that self-builders proved to be model citizens.'

It appears that the scheme was set up as a similar model to Silver Birch, with a commitment of 26 hours expected of the 15 to 20 builders, and that they had one man - Fred Moore - who was good with figures managing the finances. They encountered similar problems valuing their houses for each stage of their mortgage payments. They had decided on a house, mainly timber on the second storey, which proved very difficult to get and would create problems if an 'inept carpenter' cut the wrong length. Often a point of discussion when a group of 'worried carpenters' were observed in deep discussions, others on the build would pass the comment around: 'the carpenters are in the quog'. With a considerable amount of flourish, they managed to complete the first pair 707/709, by 20th October, 1950. An official opening took place with various eminent members of the Council: Rev. Emlyn Jones, Maurice Mell, C. R Hutchinson, Councillor W. M. Thomas, the general works manager from Dunlop and Julius Silverman MP for Erdington.

Having had a change of government, Solihull was seizing the initiative to encourage as many self-helpers to look to their district for support as they could. As such, they intensively lobbied those in central government for additional licences; it was at this point that licences were suspended in order for the new government to make a managed assessment of what actually needed doing. At the same time, many others had heard about the self-helpers making progress in Sheldon (as we know Dot regularly hosted coach-loads of visitors: the curious and the keen). These few schemes and an MP's speech raised the profile, not just locally but nationally. Locally, self-help associations were forming and seeking guidance from George Lavender's 'Central Association', then following the model and making approaches to Solihull UDC. Nationally, the picture was becoming clearer to those that mattered that this was a positive addition to the housing problem.

10. All in the scheme of things

The National Federation of Housing Association had not paid much attention to the lot of the self-help movement until the profile had become raised in the House of Commons. They may well have reviewed the act that specified government support for organisations established to support the process. It may have been at that point they made the decision that, as they were so prominently placed in London and accessible to those in government, they should be the organisation to oversee these new activities and provide steer to aspiring groups. I uncovered a file of letters from the organisation (National Archive), investigating the credentials of various spurious self-help organisations that were springing up around London, Birmingham and Solihull; events that followed their investigations led to the demise of all other support organisations excepting theirs.

By the end of 1951, prior to the speech in the House, Fortitude and the four other existing schemes, including Silver Birch, were well-established on their sites and actively building and they were all seeking their second allocations of licences, which all hoped would come with the attention that the district was getting. A further six associations had formed and are minuted as having approached Solihull: Progressive, Acorn, Shirley Self Build, Supreme, Shakespeare and Avon, between them wanting to build 54, 40, 22, 40, 35 and 40 houses respectively.

Both the Progressive and the Shakespeare housing associations have also left records behind in the public library for research. Neither of these organisations were supported via employers, but were self-formed and certainly in one case over-relied on the 'Central Association' for advice and support. These were associations that were collectives of desperate and driven individuals determined to build, as they knew that this was the only way that they would have a chance of being housed.

Progressive were the first of the two associations to receive licences; Shakespeare was deferred until more licences were made available. W. C. Hiscox, a member of the Progressive scheme, wrote his unpublished account in 2003. It is entitled, 'Solihull Progressive Housing Association Ltd' (Self-Help Housing Association) and sub-titled: 'The story of the formation of the association and the building of 50 bungalows in Dovedale Avenue, Shirley, Solihull between April 1951 and December 1954'. They formed in a similar way to the other schemes, following advice from George Lavender. The land agents, as before, were Shipway and Doble who suggested land that had been previously bought by a developer at the Shakespeare Manor Estate in Shirley, Solihull. The developer had laid the site out, but had not continued post-war. The same architects that had been used for the bungalows in the Ebrington Avenue area – S. N. Cooke – were engaged, who planned a similar bungalow. Having experienced the material shortages, these were smaller and had metal window frames. But as Mr Hiscox says, to the 50 families who formed the scheme, 'they were palaces'. Once again, the Bradford and Bingley Building Society were to provide the mortgage. The members appeared drastically underfunded, as they were only expected to contribute £25 per family. They extensively lobbied Martin Lindsay for his support to intervene with Solihull in order to get the right to build, and I quote from the text the question that the MP placed before the House on the 27th November, 1951:

> "The Progressive Housing Association of Solihull should be given the permission to start building in view of the other successful schemes in the area."

He states that Harold Macmillan himself gave the response, stating that wider powers had now been given to local Councils to make these decisions.

> Of the 50 men that comprised the scheme, *(I quote Mr Hiscox):*
> "So, we had 50 members, and only four of them had ever worked on a building site before. We had a jobbing builder, 2 cabinet makers, 3 carpenters, draughtsmen, clerks, sheet metal workers, toolmakers, salesmen, milkmen, telephone engineers, upholsterer, teacher, 2 plumbers, 2 electricians, welder, optical workers, pattern maker, steel constructor, lorry driver and some specialist factory workers, but the trade we did <u>not</u> have, was a bricklayer! Indeed, we did not have a qualified bricklayer until well into our second year of building, who joined us following the resignation of an existing member… 45 of our members had served in the armed forces."

Quite a plucky undertaking from a group with very limited skill and knowledge and who were insufficiently financed.

While Progressive started on their site, Shakespeare received their first allocation of licences. There is a brief account written by a daughter of one of the families from that association in the library. 'The Shakespeare Housing Association' was written by Pamela Davies in 2005, again unpublished. She recounts a similar genesis to that of Progressive, again quoting the Fordrough Lane G.P.O. scheme and that:

> "Solihull welcomed such groups as it was a practical way of easing the housing shortage."

She writes that this group was originally formed with 36 members in 1951, but that the final number was 32 who built their houses in Portia Avenue and Fabian Crescent in Shirley. She says that 'the drop-out rate was high' on the scheme, as much due to the many miles cycled by members between where they lived/worked and the site itself. They acquired their skills from the G.P.O. Garretts Green site (I can find no evidence of this, there is no doubt that this a is a reference to Tallington Road) and they had planned to build four-bedroomed houses, but quickly realised that restrictions on materials made this economically unviable, so they built three-bedroomed houses. It took them three and half years to build thirty-two houses, and a similar points system was used to allocate priority to members of the scheme.

As was to be expected, Progressive got into difficulties early on. Mr Hiscox recalled that:

> "Progressive struggled to meet early costs and soon went into debt. They managed with much persistence to be granted a loan via Solihull UDC Works Loan Board… They arranged a loan of £62,500 (£1,250 per house). They were £6,000 in debt by august 1952 when the loan came through. They had started 14 properties and 2 were ready with the roof on."

According to Solihull UDC Housing Committee minutes of the 11th June 1952, complaints had been received about the Central Association, that according to the Clerk, was responsible for initiating four out of the five schemes in the Sheldon area. The opinion was that at that time some difficulties had been experienced with:

> "…getting information, including rent calculations, from time to time relations on the whole had been completely satisfactory."

However, the Progressive Housing Association had made a formal complaint to the Council that they had not been properly informed of their financial commitments to a scheme before commencement by the Central Association. Subsequently, they had contacted Martin Lindsay MP:

10. All in the scheme of things

> "…who was of the opinion that investigations should be made into the financial positions of all Self-Help Groups in order to ascertain that their members would not have to pay an increased rent over a number of years owing to mounting charges made by the Central Association."

It appears from this minute that the Central Association (created and run by George Lavender) was levying charges against any association that he was assisting: as we know, George Lavender was now working freelance and had to raise an income.

Indeed, the National Federation of Housing Associations had been quite active on seeking as much information as possible on what it was beginning to identify as potentially rogue associations. It is important to point out that, through these investigations, all involved came to the conclusion that George Lavender knew more than most and was very plausible. However, Central had come to the NFHA's attention and it appears that Central would not survive this scrutiny, as the following autumn the Progressive Housing Association had become affiliated to the National Federation of Housing Associations, had applied for another 8 licences and, under the advice of the Federation, was no longer a friendly society but had become incorporated (Progressive Housing Association Ltd). Additionally, they had applied for a loan from Solihull under the 1936 Housing Act for the sum of £15,000, 'in respect of the 12 bungalows now being erected."

According to Mr Hiscox, this was by far the greatest problem that the association encountered, but they did experience many of the other difficulties common to self-help associations. The work was arduous without the aid of modern equipment, many hours spent under floodlight, digging into the Shirley clay sub-soil, which would fill after rain and would have to be bailed-out day after day. They experienced regular drain collapses and wall collapses, and were subject to the same exacting scrutiny that Silver Birch and the other schemes had encountered.

They were all affected to some extent by union problems, all of which were reported by the local press at that time - I shall discuss these articles shortly - however, they were fortunate to have many union men on their scheme and were able to smooth the waters over and obtain the materials or the electrical work that they needed. Again, as with many of the schemes, the roads were unmade until 1956 and the women would struggle with prams and the dangerous muddy conditions.

The common comment to all the schemes was that of the issues of Health and Safety (similar to the tale recounted by Pat Rowson regarding Oscar and the injury). Mr Hiscox recalls:

> "Health and Safety regulations today are very strict, but if they had been in force 50 years ago, we would never have got started!
>
>> Hard hats? No. Using hammers and chisels at heights. Ex-army boots would serve as safety boots. Secure-ish scaffolding without guard rails. Pulling trees out, 8 men and a rope!"

Back on the Fortitude scheme, they had progressed to their third allocation of licences. By now, the scheme members were into their flow of building and using whatever strategy they could to make a little more on the deal. As Silver Birch had dealt in fire-damaged bricks in order to cut cost, Fortitude had developed a system of loading their brick lorry leaving a central gangway for ease. However, from time to time, a few more bricks would fill that gangway than were actually purchased, assisted by the blind eye of 'the

10. All in the scheme of things

weighbridge operatory (sic), who knowing we were a self-help group, were invariably quite forgetful about the correct laden weight of our lorry'.

Fortitude were to finish first out of three schemes noted here. Followed by Shakespeare in early 1954 and then Progressive in November 1954. This really was the boom-time for self-help across the district. It is hard to imagine now, so much building activity in such a small area, added to by the Council house and private development that was on-going. The whole of Solihull must have been peppered with very active mini-building sites, as the minutes of Solihull UDC Housing Committee record the many schemes that they facilitated between 1950 and 1956: Rover, Lucas (U Build It), Fortitude, Silver Birch, Sparkhill, Tyburn, Shirley Self-Build, Acorn, Supreme, A.I.T., United, Cateswell, Rowood, Advance, United Effort, Lavender. It is probably because of this explosion of self-enterprise that, inevitably, the public's attention was drawn to the considered over-development of the area. I turn to the local press reporting of public opinion in 1953, which illustrates the change that was taking place in the discourse from warmth to antagonism that would mean an end to the boom of self-help locally.

1953 appears to be a monumental year in the history of Solihull for quite significant reasons; it was the year of the coronation of Queen Elizabeth II in June of that year, and the year that the district was informed that they were to be granted their Charter of Incorporation as a Borough, thus assuring a new status and the ability to fend off any further land encroachment from the city of Birmingham.

Initially in the press, there was encouragement towards the perception of Solihull's activities in promoting and achieving development, praise for the issuing of mobile licences for 'little home' (Solihull and Warwickshire County News-3.1.53), and promotion of how Solihull had not just built many council houses in the last year but also outstripped many urban centres in their achievements. Solihull had completed 327 houses as compared to 234 in the previous year. They were estimating a further 350 houses for 1953 *(my note - a significant contribution would be made by self-help schemes)*. As was being pointed out by the Council:

"The number under construction in Liverpool is 502, in Birmingham - with a population 17 or 18 times that of Solihull - 468, in Manchester 415 and Leeds 392."
(Coun. W. M. Thomas-Solihull and Warwickshire County News-24.1.53).
It was also quoted in the same article that there were 1,100 eligible for houses, and that (significantly for this book) 709 were now 'entitled' to build houses in Solihull that had not been previously able to do. At the same time 2,000 people remained waiting on the list for houses.

However, a month before the coronation, residents in Shirley were beginning to object strongly to the plans for 200 more council houses being built in their Area *(my note - many of the self-help schemes had obtained land on the Shakespeare Manor Estate in Shirley)*. This was added to in the press that there were concerns that local services, such as schools, were becoming over-stretched by the sudden influx of new people. Further, by July 1953 the Council had their own concerns after it had been reported that Birmingham and three other Councils had met in order to address the Birmingham overspill by building a new town: The Council were disgruntled as they had not been informed. The Council made their objections firmly, citing the fact that they had done much to absorb this over-spill, particularly because:

111

10. All in the scheme of things

> "Under the self-housing scheme more than 500 houses had been or were being built in the Solihull District and of these 98 per cent would be homes for Birmingham families."
>
> *(Solihull and Warwickshire County News-18.7.53)*

This battle continued in the press that month, with Solihull responding to criticisms from Warwickshire County Council that Solihull had not done enough.

Meanwhile, the resentment felt by contractors and building operatives towards the self-help schemes was becoming apparent, and various comments had been made that the work was sub-standard and that Solihull was effectively allowing queue jumping. Maurice Mell, who had been a great advocate of the self-help principle had responded with strength in an article in the Solihull and Warwickshire County News-1.8.53:

> "In his address, Mr Mell said that he could not help but admire those self-help builders, who, after a hard day's work, were prepared to devote their spare time to building their own houses and helping their friends to build theirs... Answering letters of criticism that the self-help associations were jumping the queue he said:
>
> "...that in his opinion, a man that was prepared to help himself was entitled to jump the queue.'"

That same month it became public that the Council had received the grant of the Charter of Incorporation (news that the Council were aware of four months previously according to the UDC minutes). In the article in the Solihull and Warwickshire County News-15.8.53, Solihull Council quoted the growth of the district to nearly 70,000 people and the fact that they had been seeking this charter as far back as 1938. This now assured the Council the right to devolved spending powers, free of County Council control.

The following month, a public enquiry was launched into the proposed development of the 200 new council houses in Shirley, followed a month later by stark warnings from the Council that a prospective 'land famine' could end the 'housing boom' in Solihull. By November, there had been firm support from the County Council for Solihull's objections to a new town being proposed by Birmingham and that there were fears that 'Solihull and Sutton Coldfield' would be swallowed up, "as Erdington and Handsworth had been in the past.'"

Solihull celebrated the Charter in 1954. For a while their support for self-help continued, as did their expressed intention to build council houses. It was the case that self-help had been redefined by many as private development, and was often used as an objection to Solihull's housing policy. Criticism of failing the homeless by supporting more private (including self-help) to Council development were frequently railed by the opposition. As the minutes of the Housing Committee testify, the vast majority of these schemes received the subsidised support to enable them to build, and it was due to the changes in national policy that enabled those builders to buy. All of the self-help schemes had been comprised of individuals that were simply desperate enough to endure hardships to build a council house that they would not be entitled to through waiting; as we know, many had no intentions of being house owners, they were just grateful to have a home.

The national wave of home building was stimulated by much that occurred in Solihull, and is often cited in the numerous publications that the National Federation of Housing Association <u>sold</u> to its very large membership. Many enterprising little schemes sprung up, particularly in the London area, but also in many other urban centres and some

10. All in the scheme of things

rural locations around the country. All were made aware of what the G.P.O. workers had done in Birmingham and how significant it had become to the government of the time.

With a change of government in 1955, it was decided that the national housing programme had served its purpose: slum clearance and new town creation was being addressed, and the critical shortage that had been faced in 1945 had subsided substantially. The council house subsidy was withdrawn. This marks the shift in Local Authority policy, and in Solihull's case the other significant happening of incorporation and boundary protection had also served to create a thriving borough. The last schemes were being approved for land there in 1957. In April 1958, this minute marks the end of self-help in Solihull:

> "The Borough surveyor submitted two enquiries as to whether the Council to lease land to newly formed Housing Associations for the erection of a limited number of dwellings by their members.
>
> Resolved-That the Council regret that they have no land available for lease to any other Housing Association."

It was the end of an era, a time when all worked for an eventual aim, maybe not necessarily the same end goal, but an aim that would achieve prosperity. The Council were able to oversee the future development of an independent town that would go from strength to strength, eventually obtaining Metropolitan Borough status, with a prosperous infrastructure and outlook; to the envy of many of its neighbours. The people that flocked there in their hundreds were able to make lives for themselves that were far removed from anything that they could have possibly dreamed of in the aftermath of World War II and the crippling years of austerity that had followed. I feel that the last words of this story should be from those schemes that have left record, other than Silver Birch, as a celebration to all the many schemes that undertook this amazing adventure. Pamela Davies (2005) reflects this enormity when she writes:

> "Today, when you read of Self-Help building schemes in the press, it usually refers to a group of people, who have come together to provide themselves, with homes, but who employ tradesmen to do the hard flog. I think it was a marvellous thing that the men who belonged to the Shakespeare Housing Association were able to build their houses while still keeping their daytime employment. It will be sad if this groups achievement is forgotten."

And W. C. Hiscox (2003) ends his account with a simple but powerful statement that sums it up for the hundreds of families locally and the thousands nationally, when he writes:

> "The spirit of comradeship has been returned over the years and pride in the fact WE MADE IT HAPPEN!"

Part 3

'When needs drive'

Chapter 11

Reflections of the past

They say there is no such thing as a new idea, all things inevitably repeat. It may be that they appear as other things, disguised in different terms and circumstances, but invariably what we see has been in some form before. This is true of the 1950's self-help movement, although the words 'self-help' apply to a very different concept today: that being the idea of changing one's life for the better, either materially, or mentally; getting up and doing something that effects a change in our circumstances through physical efforts, or changing our mind-set towards a more positive frame of thinking and existing. The self-help of the 1950's has become the self-build of today, and that too, has taken on many different forms, from the custom (high-end) self-build, through to the lower-end, small project of an individual nature, generally on a tight budget. The whole spectrum of the individual project has been widely publicised through programmes on television such as the long-running Channel 4 programme 'Grand Designs' hosted by the enigmatic talent of Kevin McCloud.

Fantastic projects reminiscent of the title with enormous budgets, architects of note (and not), advanced materials and technologies, in prominent (expensive) areas, allow us all insight into what can be possible if one has the wherewithal that is not constrained to the basic necessity of living. It is fair to comment that even those medium-range and lower-end projects require a substantial amount of basic capital that is either raised through the sale of an existing property, then further enhanced through other finance streams, or a substantial mortgage that has to be raised to offset the cost of the build. These routes are beyond the reach of first-time buyers, and these are often the people desperately seeking homes.

It is well-reported that many young people are remaining under their parents' roofs for longer and longer. The cost of renting can be prohibitive for many, never mind the prospect of buying a property. For some time before this practice forfeited financial subsidy, some parents of students in higher education used the opportunity (if capital were available) to buy a low-end property for a shared rental amongst a group of students, thus building equity for their son or daughter to offset costs. However, with the escalating costs of Buy-to-Let mortgages, the downturn in university applications due to high tuition fees (in the UK, not Scotland), and the over-heated housing market (particularly true the further south that you travel), this practice has all but died out.

Many other young people cannot aspire to higher professional incomes, as they are turning away from higher education routes in favour of paid employment; the cost of tuition fees has created a very pragmatic generation. Consequently, their level of income is set too low even for the rental market in many areas; this is even more pronounced in rural areas, where second-home ownership is prevalent. These youngsters have no choice but to remain with their parents longer and longer, even into their mid-thirties, before they are able to seek another, more independent, lifestyle. This does change their aspirations for marriage and

11. Reflections of the past

family, and delay many of these life choices until they may become affordable and independence be assured.

Rural locations and exclusive urban areas are particularly prohibitive for finding alternative, independent living for the younger generation. The more rural, picturesque, beautiful, or popular a location, the more expensive the market has become. Land prices have escalated to unbelievable levels, as the clamour for second-homes by those in position to buy, has increased. Some areas of the UK can be sixteen times more expensive than similar locations further north. This has the knock-on effect of pushing up house prices substantially and prohibitively in those areas, even for the local working income. Young people just starting life have simply no chance and no opportunity to ever be able to aspire to property ownership in those locations, and in many cases, are unable to afford local rented accommodation, as the artificially higher than normal house prices are reflected in the private-rental market.

This has caused many young people to have to move away from locations where generations of their family have existed, and has been mourned by many villages; the death of the village, the loss of young people, the arrival of artificial numbers of 'outcomers' and retirees. Exclusive urban areas have seen similar population shifts, most notable in London, where traditional working-class areas have begun to become fashionable, forcing house prices upwards (as the housing-bubble moves further and further out).

Some of the problems have been addressed through sheltered housing projects, peppercorn rents, shared-ownership, and subsidies that have come from central government in the form of tax relief in various ways for first-time buyers. The problem is that we have been facing a monumental housing crisis for thirty years, and those strategies that are being employed are simply not enough to make a substantial difference. That is why the new attention to self-build, that began to be highlighted under the last coalition government, has appeal, as it could offer the opportunity for many, not only to own their own property, but additionally to remain in the location where their family-networks are.

In this part of the book, which consists of three chapters, I am going to explore the reasons why I believe the housing crisis of recent years continues to be a persistent problem. I will highlight some of the raft of legislation and support networks that can be exploited by those who wish to do it for themselves, and I hope to demystify the process for those eager to try. In the final chapters, I will tell the story of two modern-day self-build schemes, very reminiscent of the endeavours of Silver Birch. Again, I will use the words of those who have actually done it to tell their own story.

We can trace the roots of the current housing crisis back to the mid 1980's. This was the time of 'Thatcherism' as it has been coined; the time when the Conservative government, under the leadership of Margaret Thatcher, followed the doctrine of privatisation and deregulation. The thrust of the political philosophy under the Conservatives between 1979 and 1990 was a move away from the post-war agenda of the collective welfare state and economy. The Thatcherites believed in the free market economy and denationalisation. In order to gain support with the traditional working-class majority (who were suffering the effects of trade union restriction and de-nationalisation and closure of industries such as coal) the idea of home ownership through the 'Right-to-Buy' was promoted heavily. It was decided to release the council house stock from Local Authority control, thus enabling the tenant the right to purchase their home at a much-reduced market value. Additionally, this enabled local authorities to raise revenue for other projects, and contributed to the national treasury; those traditional Labour authorities that would have been fundamentally opposed were keen to accept the financial inducement from the sales of their Council housing stock, as they were facing their own curb in funding from central government. It had been promoted as giving the tenant the right to own their own a home and relied on a British tradition of home-ownership (which as we know historically is a relatively modern invention). Consequently, it was a move away from a social state.

Council houses were offered at between 33% and 50% less than their current market values in the mid-1980's to the tenants; 1 in 3 took the opportunity and 200,000 houses were sold in a relatively short time. This initial sell-off continued at a more modest figure in the 1990's, and the rules were modified from 2005, stipulating that a tenant must have inhabited a home for a minimum of 5 years before the Right-to-Buy would be made available to them.

The statistics of that release of the stock (keeping in mind the massive council house building programme of the late 1940's to the 1960's) was that 1 in every 3 houses was a council house prior to the 1980's. The figure given now is that only 1 in 10 houses is a council house. Although much revenue has been raised over the last 30 years of selling off these houses, very little proportionally has been used to replace housing stock that has been sold off. However, the route that has been exploited is the support of the registered Housing Association.

The new Housing Associations are not to be confused with those wonderful groups of men from the 1950's; these new bodies are very formal and very professional, they are generally highly experienced operatives from the construction industry and work as systematic and organised enterprises. Under the terms of the 1985 Housing Act, they are still not-for-profit and are either formed via trust deeds, co-operatives, as provident societies, or as registered charities. Having a not-for-profit status and following the requirements of providing homes for disadvantaged groups within society, has enabled them to access government funding and subsidies in order to operate as formal organisations, employing staff and manpower. Their brief is to provide sheltered accommodation, shared-ownership, and tenanted-homes to such groups as: the disabled, low-income families, those with learning disabilities and mental health issues, those that have suffered from substance abuse, ex-offenders, refugees, and women fleeing domestic violence.

They are no longer viewed as being connected to the current self-build movement: this I confirmed by placing a Freedom of Information request to every planning authority in England. In this request, I asked each authority whether they had any housing associations on their register for Custom and Self-Build. Housing associations are separate and distinct from this register and do not have to register as such, however, many authorities took great pains to inform me that they did indeed have housing associations active in their areas providing these needed homes.

Why then, with such activity, are we still facing a huge housing shortage?

There are a combination of factors that exist, that are due to the social and economic changes within society, that have led to raised levels of aspiration, levels of income, and by that, a greater proportion of second-home ownership. Briefly, whereas my parents and their peers were just grateful to build a home to live in, so much so, that they never sold or moved on, then by changes of fortune they were able to own these homes. The society of today has been encouraged to better themselves further. The dream of living or retiring by the sea, or to some rural idyll, has become a reality for many as their income generation and certain tax advantages have accumulated.

Those with the surplus money, or who have managed to increase their savings and equity (through the rising prices of the property market), have made their aspiration a reality: second-homes have become common place either through prudent management of finances, or the inflation in house prices. Referring back to my previous comment, this is a great disadvantage for the many young people in these generally rural locations (such as Devon, Dorset, the south coast, East Anglia and Yorkshire), as the local housing market becomes over-heated, pricing the first-time purchaser out of the equation. There are also areas of the country, such as the Home Counties, London and some rural areas of the Midlands, that have become price-prohibitive; especially in London where the financial industry has attracted many to work and take advantage of the lucrative incomes. This hedonism and aspiration combined with a rising population within the UK - in 1945 it was just over 49 million, and has risen to over 64 million today - added to by the housing profile where second-homes and multiple home ownership (buy-to-let previously) have become commonplace, have further diminished an already overstretched, and under-supplied housing stock.

Consequently, as this stock of available houses has reduced more and more, so the demand has risen in some areas – that are considered more desirable or fashionable than others – the property values have escalated out of proportion to the equivalent homes available in other less attractive/popular areas. The common phrase is that your house is only worth what someone else will pay for it, and indeed this is true: the more demand there is in a local area (and the less available property), the more dramatically those house prices and the attached land values rise. Land values for the equivalent size of plot and similar location can vary substantially from the southern tip of Cornwall to the more northern parts of England, mid and north Scotland; as much as sixteen times more the further south you go. The average available plot of land for sale in Solihull these days is £200,000 (the most expensive at present is £550,000) simply impossible for any first-time buyer to consider. Compared to the time of my parents, working with the rise in inflation, that figure would have been the equivalent of £1000 to them; they struggled to raise £50. In Cornwall, the average price of a plot of land is £150,000 and can be as much as £370,000, once again not an option for a young family.

Since 1990, successive governments have tried to address the shortfall in the housing stock. With conflicting political ideologies and differing social strategies, added to by varying degrees of recession, differing priority has been placed on which sectors should be of primary importance. There is no doubt that without the emphasis of the housing association model, many sectors of society (the disadvantaged and the vulnerable) would be without adequate housing; these were those that traditionally suffered in society and were previously catered for under the social housing (council house model). However, there is now a high proportion of others who are not in serious need, or disadvantage, that have been quite simply priced out of the housing market. They may earn moderate (or in some cases professional) incomes, and may have saved judiciously, but with the cost of local housing and the inability to raise favourable mortgages because of a lack of disposable income (combined with the over-priced private housing available and the lack of suitable private, or council rental properties), they are not able to afford to get that first foot on the property ladder. Again, many of these individuals would have been housed traditionally under the social housing model if that stock had been replaced at the time that a need to re-invest should have been addressed. It has been a consideration by some governments that a private/public finance structure may help to ease the situation. However, due to recession – the construction industry always becoming one of the casualties of any recession – it has become increasing difficult to find developers willing to take on such tasks. The developers who are in operation are assured of work through the housing association model, who in turn are able to apply for, and draw down, government funding; local authorities remain on very tight budgets, unable to invest in the social housing model and so have no call to employ developers.

Land prices at times have soared, and equally, when there has been a down-turn economically, frozen, very often leaving developers with purchased tracts of land that – because the value of the land has stagnated and was purchased during a rise – become unprofitable to develop unless the demand in that area for property at the pre-recession values increases.

The statistics collated by the government for house building in the UK over the last thirty years make interesting reading. Whereas private development has remained between 100,000 and 200,000 a year depending on the fluctuations in the economy, housing associations began to feature as significant in the 1980's and have averaged 30,000 homes per year over the last ten years. This is in stark contrast to the Local Authority social house building, which at the beginning of the 1970's was 185,000 per year, dropping to 89,700 in 1979/80, 19,380 in 1989/90, and declining rapidity to 320 per year at the turn of the millennium. At its lowest point in 2004, only 130 Local Authority houses were built across the whole of the UK. In the last 10 years, there has been a slight increase year on year, but house building by local authorities can now be counted in the thousands rather than the hundreds of thousands. In 2015/16, 3,030 houses were built by local authorities. This decrease in house building overall has had a detrimental effect on the industry as a whole; with less operatives required, so less apprentices have been trained, as many workers were laid off during the most recent global recession. With so few having been trained, we are now facing an acute national skills-shortage.

Much of what is happening now is a mirror of the mid 1940's though for very different reasons. The government estimates from 2015 were that 232,000 and 300,000 homes were needed a year, a similar story to the monumental years featured earlier in the book. What Hitler and the urgent slum-clearance necessitated then, so a dearth of available affordable property, either to rent or buy, is achieving now. There is no doubt that the UK has suffered as the world has with the recent economic downturn, however, we are not in the same calamitous financial straits that we were seventy years ago, which begs the question, why could the government manage to deliver the needed homes over the decade of 1945 to 1955, yet we are barely building at all now?

This is not the book to discuss the convoluted fiscal policies of successive governments. However, if we observe that back in 1946 we had an 'infant' Welfare State and National Health System, and now we have a well-established entity, with a rapidly ageing population, and with many within our population benefiting from health technologies and advancements that have simply out-stripped the capacity to fund; it is not hard to make a leap to the understanding that with a finite amount of available money that can be raised through taxation, priorities of health, education and social care, tend to merit greater importance than

11. Reflections of the past

that of housing at a national level. At a local district council level, again much-reduced funding over many years from central government, combined with the needs to deliver a multitude of essential services, infrastructure, and education to local council tax payers, means that there is no money to develop houses.

In 2015 parliament reported that it envisaged that by 2020, because of the ever-increasing gap between the level of disposable income and the increasing cost of houses, 'home ownership would be impossible for those not already on the ladder'. From the statistics of the housing market by tenure then, it was stated that since the 1990's outright home-ownership had decreased from 44% to just above 30%, and that those with an outstanding mortgage had risen from 25% to 33% and was continuing to rise. Further, that due to a lack of social housing, social renters had declined from 24% to 17%, and the private rental sector in that period had doubled from 10% to 20% and was set to continue to rise at the same rate. The Office for National Statistics reported in their bulletin of March 2017 that:

> "On average, working people could expect to pay around 7.6 times their annual earnings on purchasing a home in England and Wales in 2016, up from 3.6 times earnings in 1997."

And further:

> "The median price paid for residential property in England and Wales increased by 259% between 1997 and 2016; median individual annual earnings increased by 68% in the same time period."

Although between 2010 and 2015 the housing association market was in a stronger position and meeting some Local Authority shortfall, there had been a cut in government spending to both housing associations and local authorities for housing from £8.4 billion to £4.5 billion. At the same time, due to uncertainties of the proposed welfare reforms that were on-going, the new round of funding (that had once again declined to £3.3 billion) had been well received by housing authorities, but they were more cautious to commit; their clients may well be affected by cuts in benefits, meaning that demand for the housing that housing associations may develop would decline also.

For the 2015 general election, the main parties stated their manifesto pledges to address the housing problem. The Conservatives were keen to extend the 'Right-to-Buy' to housing association members, and build 200,000 Starter Homes. Labour promised to build 200,000 homes per year by 2020. The Liberal Democrats held by their principle of delivering 300,000 homes per year, with a plan to address the housing crisis presented within their first year of government, if they were to be elected. As we know, the Conservatives are now in government (*My note – this chapter was written in March 2015*) and have other pressing matters such as another General Election and BREXIT to contend with. Consequently, their plans for the housing situation have in some ways become obscured by the important issues of the now. Following the announcement of the upcoming General Election for June 2017, and in order to update my findings, I have reviewed current party pledges; once again the major opposition parties are promising a million homes or more in the term of their parliament (Labour insists that half of those should be in Local Authority ownership), and the Conservatives are currently applying their existing strategies enacted since 2015, that I continue to discuss in this chapter.

The Department for Communities and Local government has published a consultation for their proposed Housing White Paper, 2017, "Fixing our Broken Housing

Market". In her introduction, Theresa May has written that in the last 10 years the ratio of the prices of houses to the average income has doubled; more dramatically, average costs are now 8 times that of average income. Of those, 2.2 million working families now find that their disposable income is insufficient to pay a third or more towards housing. In order to address these problems, the government is offering a raft of solutions to promote greater housing development, including: simplifying the planning regulations further, while enabling more revenue to be gained by planning departments through the raising of fees; assisting the construction industry by offering various financial incentives to build; addressing training for the skills-shortage, giving greater financial support to housing authorities to encourage more development; identifying available land for building; encouraging the custom-builder; and seeking to support the SMEs within the construction industry. All that is addressed in this consultation is very praise-worthy and is added to the raft of legislation that I have mentioned in my introduction to this book; the 'Garden-Towns', the 'Right-to-Build', the 'Right-to-Buy', the new 'Starter Home' strategy, and various supports to help first-time buyers access the housing ladder.

One could argue that there are so many policies that some conflict with others, and there is the risk that good housing strategies become obscured (or confused) in the myriad of alternatives. There is also a question of land availability, and the prices of that land. The Conservatives were clear when they published their manifesto that they would protect the land within any greenbelt and that they continue to do. There are two conflicting arguments over greenbelt land; two-sides of the fence. One says that it is more in line with environmental and climate concerns to conserve and protect greenbelt; the other, that there is a work-related, social need for housing within localities and it is more environmentally damaging to use transport to travel to and from places of work. Their argument follows that it is 'greener' to develop on that greenbelt; of course, that has a knock-on effect of increasing urban-sprawl and decreasing houses prices in that locality. Traditionally, greenbelt land has been in constituencies where property values are high, and the presence of a greenbelt assures those high values.

An unfortunate casualty of this latest housing reform through lack of profile, has been the absence of a vision first promoted under the Labour government of 2008 and then championed under the last coalition government - Community Land Trusts. This concept arose from the United States Civil Rights movement, whereby community-centred collectives were formed to manage local land and housing assets. The idea was then adapted in the UK by other groups with similar interests during the 1990's.

A wide consultation took place in 2008 and the government of the day realised the potential for generating self-build social housing stock through this model. They proceeded to raise various pieces of legislation to ensure retention of that stock, and assistance for those groups to raise finance and afford suitable building plots. The coalition government that followed were particularly keen to support the self-build and custom-build policy for addressing the problems of housing, and the role of the CLT was part of that sphere and was supported in strength. A number of strategies were employed in order to raise awareness of these avenues of housing development including the appointment of Kevin McCloud as a champion for self-build and custom, and nominating 12 vanguard districts to pilot these strategies. Additionally, an Act was passed in 2015 - the Self-Build and Custom

11. Reflections of the past

Housebuilding Act - that stipulated that each planning authority in England and Wales must keep a register of all those with expressed interest to self or custom build.

The concerns at the time were that the UK was somewhere behind those in Europe, where self-build has been considered the norm and a positive way of providing much-needed housing stock. The evidence drew from published statistics and various academic sources that compared the UK to other parts of Europe; it reveals that very little self-building occurs within England and Wales (Scotland has always been more proactive in this area). As we know from the earlier chapters of this book, in Sweden and the rest of Scandinavia, self-build is a common-place activity, and is often undertaken by extended families of the builder. In Austria, as another example, self-build is estimated to account for 80% of all housing development; in France, 60%. Much interest at that time and since has been directed towards a revolutionary scheme that has emerged in The Netherlands in a town called Almere (east of Amsterdam). Following a Dutch National Housing report in 2001 entitled 'Mensen, Wensen, Wonen', that suggested that by 2040 one third of Dutch housing should be built by self-build, the politicians in Almere set out to prove that a large scale self-build development was possible, and they invested in 1,500 serviced plots to attract custom self-builders. The pilot scheme has been well-received, and has attracted many to establish their dream home. Although the brief was to attract as much low-cost affordable housing as possible, the flexibility in planning and the price of plots has led to many high-end, custom-builds being established there.

It is also true to say that 'Grand Designs', presented by Kevin McCloud, features many such properties; the vast majority of projects being single build rather than community schemes. However, one programme was aired 13th May 1999 that featured the Hedgehog Housing Association of Brighton in their co-operative build, which has attracted a lot of interest and inspired many other groups to action. A clip of this episode is available to view on: https://youtu.be/VaB_7S8cQII. This project started building in early 1998, although it had been initiated two years previously by four families. Eventually, after many hours of commitment, 10 families erected 10 family homes, that they subsequently rent through a housing association.

There is no doubt that Kevin McCloud shares this vision for sustainable, affordable, low-cost housing and that is why he was selected as the champion for self-build and custom build. Much has been made of this with his inclusion as champion on supportive websites such as 'The Self-Build Portal', which offers a 'how-to guide' for all those who wish to start on their self-build dream. Particular features of this site include a map of the UK for those seeking plots to build with their budgets displayed, and links to help the prospective builder through a long 'to do' list, whether that be the individual, or the group. Another website that features 'the champion' once again is National Custom and Self Build Association, which was initiated through the housing industry as a forum to bring together all of the information and contacts online. There are a number of other sites who actively promote assistance to the individual project.

Individual projects depend on the ability of the prospective house builder to raise the necessary finance, mainly through routes of mortgage and existing assets. But for many people this is simply not an option, as I have already discussed extensively in this chapter: they are either too young to have amassed that sort of capital, or are of an income that would never allow them to save for any large capital outlay (and meanwhile where would they live?).

11. Reflections of the past

The exorbitant cost of land and available houses, certainly in some areas, is well beyond the reach of most, hence the idea of forming a community of builders becomes more and more attractive. In the same way that my parents and many other of that generation were faced with no alternative but to do it for themselves, now with increasing awareness from the multitude of self-build promotions, many are now coming to the same conclusion. The Community Land Trust makes the impossible, possible.

In the next two chapters, I will put forward two case studies of Community Land Trusts in action. Once again, I shall use their narrative as much as possible to tell their stories. These people are making their history today for all those that will follow in the future. As much as the Hedgehog Housing Cooperative were on a steep learning curve with their own development, so too, these two stories that follow have gained much knowledge and experience that they are happy to share with the readers of this book. They are the history that has completed the circle of seventy years, out of the memory of the present generation, yet, the same problems and drawbacks faced them, and they have met each challenge head-on to successfully house those who 'did it for themselves'. These stories are about celebrating what many would consider beyond their capabilities, either through a perceived lack of skill or experience; both these narratives are the proof that anyone with the drive and the determination can build their own home. As Ken Quiney of Silver Birch said, it was because of necessity they all had to do it, and that is as true today as it was seventy years ago - 'necessity is the mother of invention'.

Chapter 12
St. Minver

By definition a Community Land Trust, according to the Housing and Regeneration Act 2008, is:

"…a corporate body which

1) is established for the express purpose of furthering the social, economic and environmental interests of a local community by acquiring and managing land and other assets in order-

   - to provide a benefit to the local community
   - to ensure that the assets are not sold or developed except in a manner which the trust's members think benefits the local community

2) is established under arrangements which are expressly designed to ensure that:

   - any profits from its activities will be used to benefit the local community (otherwise than by being paid directly to members)
   - individuals who live or work in the specified area have the opportunity to become members of the trust (whether or not others can also become members) the members of a trust control it."

Essentially, a CLT are the managers of local community-owned assets of land and houses. According to the National Community Land Trust Network, many are set up in response to the issue of providing affordable housing to stop the haemorrhage of young people from a locality. As a legal not-for-profit entity, a CLT can acquire land either through bequests or gifts, or purchase it. Community Land Trusts are quite literally the local community driven to action, members are volunteers and those willing to commit a considerable amount of their spare time (and in many cases personal expertise) to benefit those around them.

The National Community Land Trust Network state on their website that there are now over 225 CLTs up and down the country, the largest of which have over 1000 members. To date, these organisations have developed over 700 homes, and will have developed a further 3000 by 2020. These are small numbers in the scheme of the national need, but they are providing needed homes in a locality. Whatever the CLT has been constituted to do, whether it be redeveloping existing community assets, producing community-grown food, or developing new assets, all must be done without profit; any surplus must be reinvested back into the community projects. The national network directs CLTs towards accessing start-up and development funding, and helps to identify other sources of funding that may be available, either from government and local government, via the local community, grants and loans, or even crowdfunding.

12. St. Minver

It is true to say, that in 2010 the CLT model had a higher profile than it does today, and the lack of political status now may be the cause of the general lack of current public awareness that these options are available. In my collection of Local Authority information via Freedom of Information requests, I posed a question to each planning authority, asking how many Community Land Trusts each authority has registered on the Self Build and Custom register (which each planning authority is obliged to keep-however CLTs are not obliged to register). As expected, a positive response to that inquiry was very low; out of 190 replies less than 0.5% answered that they had CLTs registered, though there were 17 other groups (not registered as CLTs) throughout England.

Had this request had been made eight years ago, a more positive response may have been returned (had the data been available of course – the register was only introduced two years ago). What is clear now, is that very little is known about the activities of these groups, or indeed that there is a possibility of building homes within a community that remain 'community-owned' assets; except within the network of CLTs. It is possible to speculate that if this concept had wider promotion, and greater public awareness was generated, the idea would gain momentum, especially within those communities that I have discussed in the previous chapter, where property has become price-prohibitive for many living and working in that local community.

I was fascinated by this model, and after making contact with one or two Community Land Trusts that stood out as examples of best practice on the internet, I was fortunate enough to have responses from St. Minver and Broadhempston Community Land Trusts. These are both prime examples of communities working proactively, as they have no other choice; the former is located in Cornwall and the latter in Devon. Cornwall and Devon are considered to be two of the most expensive areas in the United Kingdom to buy property, due to extensive second home ownership. There is no doubt that the wealth that is generated by those who are drawn by the exceptional beauty and climate of the Cornwall peninsula is of considerable benefit to the Cornish economy; it is the industry of Cornwall and Devon and it attracts considerable investment. The downside, of course, is the decline of historically-established communities; as house prices rise astronomically and inevitably (and local incomes do not) so there is little choice but to leave the area.

However, the people of Rock, near Padstow, Cornwall, had a guardian angel in their midst who was concerned about the loss of the young people, as the house prices soared inevitably. Mr Bill Dingle, who was a local builder and parish Councillor, looked on in concern, as more and more homes locally were sold off to others, and the young people of the area began to leave. He was the instigator of what would become St. Minver Community Land Trust. A friend and like-minded comrade of his, Mr Dave Wills, was a gentleman farmer and landowner. He had land a plenty, which he could sell at substantial profit as the relative land-values of the area increased with the housing demand, however, he knew that something had to be done to save the village and the community that he loved. He, too, had been an active member of many parts of the community for most of his life, right up until his death in 2012; so much so, that The Cornish Guardian (21/3/12) lead with the headline of the loss of this man held so dear in the community. It is thanks to the combined efforts, devotion and philanthropy of these much-loved men that quite a number of local families have been able to build their own homes and stay in their community.

12. St. Minver

Mrs Helen Rawe, Company Secretary, St. Minver CLT Ltd., provided me with an extensive account of the 'what' and the 'how' behind this trust, and as I should, I have left her narrative unedited. They have also provided photographs to illustrate their progress and the outcomes of their labours:

Then we'll do it ourselves ...

Rock is a village on the Camel Estuary, opposite Padstow, in North Cornwall. In North Cornwall it has taken 16 times the average household income to buy a house of average value, and in Rock this figure is much higher. Reputedly one of the most expensive places in the world to purchase a home, with high levels of second home ownership and holiday lets, it has become ever more difficult, especially for young people, to stay local.

The self build answer was instigated by a local builder and parish councillor, who was dismayed to note his children's peers having to move away, unable to compete in the local housing market. He hatched a plan to do something about it, envisaging a self help effort under his supervision. Sadly he passed away prematurely, but he inspired local people to deliver on his idea, and the development is named after him. The site – provided by a local farmer and parish councillor, at a price which ensured that the properties really would be affordable (plots priced at £8,000 and £11,000) – was an exception site, outside the development boundary but close to it and to local facilities.

An informal group of six local people decided to form St. Minver Community Land Trust Limited, none of whom needed a house. The only motivation for the individuals was to help develop affordable housing in the area. The former landowner served as the chairman. Over time charitable status was achieved. Early meetings took place with District Council Planners. They initially favoured a development of terraced houses, to minimize land take and provide higher density construction, which had been the policy applied to previous 'affordable' applications locally. Planning policy had stated that Rock is characterised by large individual houses on large plots which should not be subdivided. The CLT favoured detached single storey properties, both for ease of self build and surrounding 'elbow' room. The plan which eventually received approval was for 12 detached bungalows – 8 with 3 bedrooms, and 4 with 2, each property having a garage and surrounding garden: visitors from across the country, seeking to address their own affordable housing issues, have commented favourably on the spaciousness, inside and out. These are straightforward bungalows, for ease of self build, comfortable living and affordability – the essence of the project.

Mortgages, wholly provided by the Skipton Building Society, were in the order of £78,000 and £84,000 and recognition of the self builders' labour realized the maximum 'affordable' values of £85,000 and £100,000 for 2 and 3-bedroomed properties. Open market values were £287,500 and £335,000, and 'affordable' values were geared to a percentage of that, in this case 31.3%, which also applies to future sales to qualifying people. The S.106 Agreement controls future occupancy and affordability, and these obligations have to be adhered to by all successive owners. The plots were sold to the self builders with a resale covenant, which ensures that the requirements cannot be breached, plus the added assurance of a pre-emption agreement which gives the CLT a 'first refusal' to reacquire or nominate a purchaser for a dwelling when it is sold.

The two local Parish Councils supported the concept and there was much help and advice from North Cornwall District Council (later incorporated within the unitary Cornwall Council), Cornwall Rural Housing Association (initially advisory, more involved in the second phase, building four social rented units) and the newly formed Cornwall Community Land Trust. The Council provided a £5,000 start up grant and a time limited interest free loan of £544,000, which was repaid as mortgages became available. It enabled the infrastructure to go in, a road bond to be deposited with the Highway Authority, and provided working capital: the Trust was able to purchase materials in multiples of 12, keeping the price down. The money came from the council tax raised from second homes owned in the local area. The project would have been impossible without this loan.

The CLT initially found themselves treated by organisations such as South West Water, Western Power and Cornwall Highways, like a normal developer. This caused minor problems as none of the members of the CLT were experienced developers and therefore were unfamiliar with many of the processes involved in the development process. The unique nature of the St. Minver CLT meant that organizations had no experience in dealing with such developments. Over time the approach of organizations towards the CLT development changed and improved.

Some contractors treated the CLT project differently from normal jobs; for example the local company employed to do the groundwork approached the job with a degree of flexibility over timing of work and payment because of the nature of the CLT development.

To be eligible, the self builders had to have strong local connections and an income too low to be able to buy suitable housing on the open market. The development was well oversubscribed: there were 45 applicants for 12 plots. The criteria that the future occupants had to meet was set out in the Section 106 Agreement which was agreed between the Council and the CLT. A selection criteria was developed and open meetings held. There was tremendous goodwill locally towards the project.

The successful applicants for the bungalows drew lots for 2 and 3 bedroomed properties to decide which units each was to move into. They were given the opportunity to swap units if it was agreed between the two but none of them decided to do so.

The self builders started work on the site when the local contractor had completed most of the groundwork. Rather than individuals constructing their own property, the 12, sometimes with the help of family and friends, built the 12 properties, under the direction of a retained Project Manager who assisted in the development: he gave practical building advice to the self builders, using his knowledge of the construction industry to assist in areas of the development with which others were not familiar, such as ordering the necessary building materials in multiples of 12. The presence of the Project Manager was an important factor in the success of the development. Amongst the householders who moved into the development were two masons, an electrician, a roofer, an experienced decorator, and one who was experienced and confident at DIY. They didn't all have construction skills, and a mixed workforce pitched in.

They all necessarily had day jobs, so with individuals putting in 20 hours a week most of the work went on over weekends and in the lighter evenings. It wasn't easy – it meant virtually giving up their social lives for 12 months, but it gave them their own home in their own community, and they all moved into their new homes within days of each other in time for Christmas 2008.

12. St. Minver

The development fits well with the wider community but also within the development itself. Working on each other's units throughout the building development meant that the self builders had established a community of their own by the time they moved in.

The wider community came together for the official opening celebration, donating parking, hall hire, refreshments, and a wide screen to show the recorded development – it was a wonderful occasion.

Self builder and householder Victoria Mead says the development was "The best thing I've ever done in my life! More people should do it."

The success of the project and a continuing need led to the development of a second phase. Again oversubscribed, with 26 applicants for 8 plots. Phase 2 was always going to be different. Changes in local government: the District and Borough Councils were abolished and a Unitary Authority established, and the economic situation – fewer Building Societies prepared to advance mortgages, meant a changed situation. North Cornwall District Council had earmarked funds for Phase 2: the new Cornwall Council required 4 social rented properties to be provided, and forwarded a grant of £320,000 to Cornwall Rural Housing Association, £160,000 of which (£20,000 per plot) would filter through to the CLT. Individual build costs amounted to £107,000, and applying the grant reduced that to £87,000. Mortgages were harder to come by this time, with fewer Building Societies willing to lend, and tougher criteria.

It wasn't entirely plain sailing. Mortgage uncertainties, potential delay in resolving the application for a footpath diversion threatened to jeopardize grant funding, negotiating a deed of easement to drain surface water into an existing watercourse, and an archaeological survey required a dig, which confirmed that an Iron Age settlement had occupied the site previously. Discovering Iron Age houses and artefacts is very exciting, but not really what you want where you are trying to create affordable housing! It lightened the purse by £20,000, but to great relief the findings were recorded, the site backfilled and development allowed to proceed.

Delays were exercising. Road adoption, and difficulties establishing open market values deferred mortgage drawdowns.

The Project Manager from the first phase agreed to take the same role for the second phase. As before, the self builders worked as a team, and materials purchased in bulk to keep costs down.

Moving into the units was a mixture of families but also single people. Single men rarely qualify for alternative types of social and affordable housing, the Council and other organizations prioritising families with children. As a result of providing for single people to move in to the development the CLT has managed to cater for a section of the population not normally assisted by housing developments, as well as helping to maintain a community of mixed people locally.

Again the official opening was magnificently supported. These two projects had shown that local people taking a hands on approach can make it happen! Truly, if every community did something similar, what a difference that would make!

Second and holiday homes continue to dominate, as in other coastal locations, but with some pockets exceeding 80%, and multi million pound values applying, action is needed to safeguard sustainable communities. There has been a prolonged search for a suitable site to accommodate a much needed third phase of self build affordable housing, an application submitted, and hopefully a positive outcome will follow shortly. Watch this space!

    The St. Minver story is encouraging and illustrates that the will to build out of necessity is still very much in existence; if people are faced with impossible circumstances that exclude all other possibilities, this is the only avenue left for many. St. Minver have to date successfully completed two phases of building within their community, and they are currently in the process of commencing phase three. I would like to draw your attention to a wonderful film about the trust from a few years ago: by watching that film you will get a sense of the huge undertaking that this group have been involved in and continue to evolve. https://vimeo.com/23261958

    In the next chapter, we will consider the story of Broadhempston. Whereas the story of St. Minver is a narrative after the event, the story of Broadhempston has been recorded for posterity in the form of a journal or diary of events.

Figure 33 – St. Minver Phase 1*

Figure 34 – St. Minver Phase 1*
- **"With grateful thanks to St. Minver Community Land Trust."*

Figure 35 – St. Minver Phase 1*

Figure 36 – Artist – Alan Caswell**
*"With grateful thanks to St. Minver Community Land Trust."
**"With grateful thanks to St. Minver Link and Martin Broadfoot."

Figure 37 – Electrician – Dan Bosley**

Figure 38 – St. Minver Phase 2*

**"With grateful thanks to St. Minver Link and Martin Broadfoot."
*"With grateful thanks to St. Minver Community Land Trust."

Chapter 13

Broadhempston

The Broadhempston Community Land Trust in Teignbridge, Devon, is a much smaller group than St. Minver, though no less committed. The narrative provided to me by one of the members – Gavin - is extensive and could be the beginnings of a book. It is a very detailed account of where it all started for him and his wife Serena and their family. I have taken the liberty of drawing an outline of the build itself, concentrating more on how this project came into existence and the various hurdles they had to jump to reach their completion in 2016. Like St. Minver, they do have a film online to view; in fact, they have been very active in publicising their project, and I suggest that you look at the Broadhempston Facebook page, as well as their very slick website https://broadhempstonclt.com/. They have a wonderful film there called SWIMBY https://youtu.be/hBToqBnrUwM (Something Wonderful in My Backyard), that really evokes the spirit of the larger family that they have become by undertaking this enormous effort together. As there are so many images online, and photographs in a book fail to capture the spirit or the constant on-going evolution, I suggest that you visit one of the sources to view their extensive visual record. They are as a group very informal and use first names, as such this narrative will reflect that and wherever possible I will use Gavin's words unedited.

According to the website, Broadhempston CLT will own the freehold of the land and 25% of the value of the houses. The self-builders own 25% by virtue of their labour and have the option either to buy the remaining 50% outright, or rent-to-buy. They do not pay rent on the 25% owned by the CLT, and should they wish to move on and sell their equity, the potential new buyer/tenant must fulfil the allocation policy of the CLT. According to Section 106 of the Town and Country Planning Act, which legislates for private agreements between local authorities and developers (in this case the CLT), it is prescribed that a given portion of the housing is affordable and fulfils a local need; as such all those who become eligible must pass certain criteria to be considered local. The land that the CLT acquired is - as with St. Minver - a Rural Exception Site, being situated adjacent to a boundary of Local Authority development, but not forming part of the Local Development Framework. The houses now built are of timber and straw-bale construction; they are very environmental, benefitting from a glass atrium that heats the house effectively, as well as being well-insulated and equipped with solar panels.

Gavin, Serena and their children are one of the six families that form this particular CLT - otherwise known as the Easterways project. The story of this inspirational group starts for Gavin in 2012, after he and his wife had moved back to their home village after living elsewhere and were struggling to find somewhere affordable to live upon their return. Initially, the idea had been formulated by a facilitation group in the region supported by the parish council, they were able to set about the process of attempting to secure the land and finance, and fulfil the application to the Local Authority under Section 106. However, from an auspicious start not all was plain sailing as we shall read:

"BCLT.   PLANNING STAGES.

August 2012
We were told about a vacancy in a Broadhempston housing project by my father-in-law Roger who is on the parish Council; he thought it might be worth us checking it out. He told us the chairman of the project was a chap called Geoff, also on the parish Council. All our children are friends in the village school and my wife and Geoff's wife Sybille knew each other through school. We arranged a quick visit to see if it was of any interest to us.
Geoff is a very quiet, intelligent gentleman (the kind you don't swear in front of) and he dutifully showed us the plans for 6 affordable, straw bale structured houses, set in 2 acres of land with an orchard, pond, possible play area for the kids and car parking designed by Andrew, an architect from Totnes. It all looked very interesting. As it turned out, Geoff told us that the land proposed to be purchased and built on was owned by Serena's Mum's cousin. Geoff mentioned we might be a good addition, since we had connections to the land owner…
We were told that there was to be an allocation policy on the spare place to ensure that whoever got the space would be from within the village envelope in order to be entitled to join the project. We have many family members in the village, our children go to the local school and Serena worked in the area, so we felt that we scored quite high on entitlement…
Happily, we were accepted over another local man who wanted to be on the project. Since we are a family, and he was a single man, it was given to us as the project was really developed for 3/ 4 bedroomed properties with families in mind."

"*September 2012 to February 2014*
We spend the next 18 months meeting in a pub back room once or twice a month, basically making plans with no real structure and no real idea what the way forward was… We talked about something called the Section 106 which is a planning obligation of the Town and Country Planning Act which makes a development proposal acceptable in planning terms, also referred to as developer contributions or community infrastructure levy. It was decided our play area would be a public facility so all the local kids could play in it. This would be our contribution instead of a financial one which, since we were trying to be affordable, would be difficult. This threw up more things for us to sort out as we had to design the play area for consideration and find someone to help us to build it within acceptable safety standards for children and insurances for public liability."

At this stage, the group were in their infancy; making baby-steps, a little naïve and being advised by a well-meaning facilitation organisation that seemed, on the surface, to understand the expectations that were being placed upon them to help this disparate group in Teignbridge in succeeding with their lofty ambitions. However, there were some moves forward made, such as: guiding the prospective self-builders towards a college course, offering an architect's design for their build, and commencing with the paperwork for the Local Authority. Some estimates of costs had been made, and a finance group – Resonance - had been involved, however, the estimates between the various parties as to what was needed varied considerably:

13. Broadhempston

"I really didn't understand any of the finance talk apart from the loan was proposed to be £650,000. Divided by 6 houses, this was just over £108k plus interest which was the cheapest 4 bedroom detached house in 2 acres of land I was likely to get. That was all I needed to understand... However, to me, a £150k 4 bed house is still the cheapest in our village by £200k so we were still happy."

"February 2014

The day of the college course we were so excited. We met with our instructors, a renewable energy expert who shows us round the latest technology and a plumber who was to teach us. We also did a health and safety test...

Yep it's all happening, I was telling friends and family, there have been a few shaky moments but we are on...

...Few days later.

Emergency meeting was called and we had no idea why!"

Everything began to unravel at this stage. The architect was not happy with the build design being of a straw-bale construction and wanted a timber-framed structure to form an integral part of the design and raised this as a duty of care with his clients. This had further ramifications being as there was no agreed design, no money could be raised against it, the financier was already losing its patience with the facilitation group and their quantity surveyors estimates. Broadhempston were suddenly on their own with no guidance, no money, and no architect. They knew they had to pull together to get things done:

"We have a choice to try and salvage this ourselves or just abandon it all and walk away. Team meeting: "What do we need to do?"

We need to form a proper committee made up of experienced people. We need help in the form of people who can step in and act as directors for our company. Fantastically we roped in Roger, self-employed farmer/fencing contractor/man of mystery /father in law, (his fault we are involved anyway!!); Philip, retired real estate specialist; the dad of Harriet, one of the self-builders; and Richard, retired headmaster and overall chairman and lord commander of all our meeting, bringing a large dose of professionalism to our meetings.

We had our board members who could help us guide our way back to Resonance and the money to build our homes.

Jonny Bray, a friend of Harriet's and accountant and mathematic whizz, put together the finance repayment package format that we needed to show Resonance how we were planning on paying them back...

Meetings now stepped up from pub to Philip's house where we now conducted ourselves by taking the minutes and working through the agenda. If we strayed off the conversation path Richard would bring us back to the relevant points that needed to be discussed. We were put into teams: Finance was Harriet and Andrea's, Media was Serena, Philip and José's. Scott, Simon and I were involved in getting quotes. Hugo worked alongside the architect and did an awful lot of planning. Geoff volunteered to be site manager, an unenviable task but with his unflappable calm nature he was the best man for that job. Things happened fast from that moment: we had Resonance back on, due in no small way to the work of Richard and Philip, plus the architect was in play too, designing a new house with timber frame instead of the structural straw which was the cause of the collapse of our project in the February...

We got the loan in October 2014 and purchased the land shortly after. We had a consultant builder, Toby, all lined up to construct the foundations and put in the service pipework, the new timber frame design had been accepted by the planning office, and a timber frame company had been contracted to do the construction of the frame.

Now all we had to do was: services, roofing, windows, doors, insulation, electrics 1st fix, plumbing 1st fix, cladding, rendering, plastering, joinery, 2nd fix plumb and electrics, screeding, flooring, put in some bathrooms and kitchens, painting and get the bloody things signed-off by the build inspector.

In hindsight, we never focused on house and design, which we should have for many reasons."

"BCLT.   BUILD STAGE
OCTOBER 2014:

We had the land, the loan, a plan going forward, but with all the fuss getting to this stage I feel, looking back, that we hadn't really looked at the house design because we were so focused on the issues of getting the land and we were very conscious of the very real fact that, at any moment, the project could fall apart. Most people have already sourced their money and have the land before going to the architects to have a designed property, which they would scrutinise over for months to get things exactly how they wanted them; we on the other hand, had essentially inherited the design. It looked good so that was all we had in the sense of involvement. We were also very conscious that any more delays could still make the project fail, as we were time critical to get started, so we basically accepted the design, because having a house with possibly a few snags is better than not having a house at all. Sounds crazy now but that was where we were...

Geoff had stepped up into the position of site manager, a reluctant hero if ever there was one. He has made huge sacrifices with his own career and family life to enable him the time to be on the build most of the time. He dealt with every problem as it arose in a calm, analytical way, with Hugo alongside dealing with much detail work, as he was previously working as an architect assistant to the architect involved in the project. Hugo has taken the year off to complete this project alongside his architectural studies. The hardworking pair has become the backbone of our project.

NOVEMBER 2014

So we owned a 2 acre field, taking possession at the beginning of November 2014. Just in time for a celebration on fireworks night…

Our welfare facilities had to be in place before commencement of the build. This will usually be, on a regular professional building site, a chemical porta loo, a place to eat in and to dry clothes, and access to hot and cold water. We also required a container for the storage of tools and equipment. The porta loo would normally be delivered on site and, whenever needed, a truck with a hose will turn up to pump out all the poo and replace with more fresh smelling chemical: it will come up once a week and empty it. Job done! However, we had a different plan of action. This was to build a compost toilet which was an elevated platform out of four, long, locally sourced tree trunks. We would then make a frame 1 metre high, pop on the walls, floor, roof, bang in some stairs, chuck some straw bales underneath it. We even utilised the old abandoned water trough that was left in the field, turned it upside down and cut in 2 bum sized holes, fixed some wood on for a partition wall, then fixed on a couple of toilet seats (we actually bought those) and got Alex, one of the kids, to make a couple of toilet roll holders. Ready to go. It was bonkers but it has served us well, and the two weekends we were building it were probably some of the most fun days we had, with the added benefit of getting us all geared up for the future serious work.

13. Broadhempston

> Toby the builder, and his team, started work on the road construction, which was required to be of the standard that a fire engine or ambulance would have access. Luckily, the Kingskerswell bypass was under construction and the only type of hard core for the road available was of the much better motorway standard, which we got cheap. We also needed the road for the deliveries from concrete trucks, and the crane to erect the timber frame.
>
> We got to work alongside Roger, putting in fences to separate our field from the adjoining fields, whilst Scott had located a caravan we could use as a site office. It was a 28 foot static caravan, perfect for us, and for free. We just needed a way of getting it from South Brent to our Broadhempston site some 10 miles away, all through tight country lanes as wide as the caravan itself, in some places wider. My wife's cousin Keir came up with the cunning plan to get it through, which included a low loader and 4x4 with a tow bar, six men and a chain saw, and a mini adventure with some very skilled driving through the lanes by Martin, Keir's workmate. Roger had arranged another little caravan from a Ron Greet, which we used in the beginning as a temporary office; it was old and battered, but it was free and served a purpose as our tea hut."

Having surmounted some major hurdles, they were on course to start their build, once the road had been laid and the groundworks, via Toby, had been completed. However, this was just the beginning of a considerable amount of physical effort on a piece of rural land:

> "Our first site based problem then happened: as construction of the road was starting, the water pipe was disconnected, probably by the digger. Thus, ensued a three month battle to get not just us supplied with water, but also the house down the road, who had lost his supply too. The water board came out and said, as it wasn't an official water pipe supplied by them, it wasn't their obligation to repair it, or indeed find the leak, which we couldn't find despite several attempts. We found what we thought was the leak, but a leak specialist came out and checked, only to report that, since there was no chlorine in the water when he tested it, it was just run off water from the field. Three months passed with no water. The house down the road had tapped into another source, but already our new neighbours weren't impressed with us. We were lost on what to do, especially as we had to have water for the end of the month for the builder to mix concrete and, as agreed, to supply water for the cattle due back in the field adjacent. Roger took things into his own hands and reinvestigated the area where our so-called leak expert had said wasn't the source. He found a pipe end after digging up the bank and asked me, the token plumber, to have a look. It was freezing cold, I was laying down on wet ground, up to my elbows in freezing water, and as I capped off the pipe end with numb hands, ready for us to fix the next day, I looked up to see Roger smiling away. I will never be sure if the satisfied look on his face was the overwhelming happiness from finding and fixing a big problem for the team build, or, as I suspect, the discomfort in his son-in-law's face as I struggled to get blood back into my fingers: probably a bit of both!"

> JANUARY 2015
>
> So, the road was built and the water back on, and a 150 metre long Devon bank was put in at the top end of the field by Keir and a digger. It was just in time for the builder to start with the marking out of the foundations, only to discover the road was put in the wrong angle, which was measured off the fence line, which was measured off plans, which had not taken into consideration the land by our entrance, which has a dozen garages on it, which belonged to someone else! So our measurements were out for the fence and the road by around 5 metres. In agricultural fields they are pretty general measurements, but when you are building houses and every metre is accounted for, this is a big problem. We had to go back to the land owner to say we had to move our fence further into her field because we hadn't taken enough and as we marked out the houses, house 6 was actually marked

on to the fence line and Devon bank. She had someone do some measurements and was happy with what we said, but it was a little embarrassing for us, and yet another delay. We had to move the fence and Devon bank again; the only things we had achieved and we were adjusting them already. Never mind, make your mistakes, learn from them and move on.

We had also started hedging in January, which is basically just sawing into trees and branches 90 % of the way through then just laying them down uphill to form a natural fence line. This was a hard but rewarding job. We had volunteers helping us: Jake, a 16 year-old local lad and family friend, came over every weekend with his chainsaw and enthusiasm and we really got going. It's a job we had to stop before the end of February when birds and mice and lots of little critters move in-we were under the ecologist's mitigation. It was a job that wasn't finished because we ran out of time, but we were happy with how far we got, with the view to continue after the build."

As is the way, what can seem a relatively straightforward undertaking can develop problems that are unforeseen: firstly, water pipes that they were unaware of, mistakes in marking out site lines, and then environmental hindrances. It is in some way due to their naivety that they were able to get on with what was required of them. Very often, if we actually know all of the possible complications and pitfalls in any undertaking of this nature from the outset, many of us would not even make the commitment to such a project, never mind actually commence, so it is credit to their determination and fortitude to continue come what may. That is why this CLT has proved so successful.

"FEBRUARY 2015

Planning on the houses took another turn, in the form of having plots 5 and 6 go back to the planning office to see if we would be allowed to move them further forward, as the houses had to be within 8 metres of the road due to building regulations or disabled access. I can't remember which, but it was either move the houses forward or the road back; the road was already in position, plus we thought the pond would be better off behind the house because of the flow of the ground in front, which potentially could have had flooding. This created a delay on those plots, which didn't affect anything as we weren't going to be working down there in that time frame. Starting at plot 1 and working our way down was our plan, 2 houses at a time.

Mid February, Toby the builder and his team returned to us to commence the footings, trenches and build up the foundations. We had opted for a block and beam floor instead of a concrete one, as they would cost roughly the same, but with block and beam the labour of getting in the beams would require lots of man power, so we said that we would do all the lifting of the beams and Toby would level and position them, then the blocks could be simply slotted in. It was very hard work, but we had plot one done in one day which was great going, plus making us a good saving on the budget. Within three weeks we had blocked the first 2 plots, and had the scaffold erected ready for the timber framers to arrive by end of March."

Gavin now writes an extensive account of the build itself in great detail. Each month and stage is accounted for. The enormous and tireless effort of those involved is painstakingly recalled; just reading the narrative you begin to become part of this mammoth undertaking, and all the while striving to maintain some sort of normality in their personal and family lives. As the work commenced of the actual building in March, by May it had become all-consuming as the tasks to be done grew exponentially in volume:

13. Broadhempston

"Weekend of 22nd May. Our work load had gone up to a level where it was necessary to have more time on site, so whoever was able started coming to site on Fridays, as well as Saturday and Sunday."

They had to learn each stage of the task of building a house in situ, and on-the-job. A college course in the confines of a workshop on a much smaller scale is one thing; the reality of actually doing it on site is another, additionally the college course had not taken place due to the initial collapse of the original project, they were completely dependent on their on-site consultant builder – Toby – for guidance in the beginning. Later during the roofing stages, Graeme Bell was a huge source of instruction and quality control. Ultimately one of the team, Scott was the one individual who assured the build standards were adhered to from start to finish. Where possible, they made sure they had practiced each task, or they sought guidance from one of their experts. The fitting of the windows was demonstrated by the supplier, however, after being shown what to do, the builders went on by themselves to complete the task. Sometimes they had to resort to fact-finding on the internet in order to better understand how to complete a task:

"Bank holiday Monday, we attempted to fix in the first Velux window which, after watching a YouTube video several times, was again another job we could do by ourselves."

Over the course of the following two months, they managed to get two of the plots to a finished roof height, a third almost there, while at the same time building the remaining three plots to various stages. All the time, they were learning and widening their skill base and knowledge. By this stage they were becoming skilled-roofers. There is a wonderful video on their Facebook page of those heady days on the roof, however you can sense the all-consuming effort is beginning to take its toll as Gavin recalls:

"With everybody working so hard it was inevitable that we start getting tired. Most of us by now had been working full time jobs and working evenings on site, plus the weekends, for the best part of 4 months with no end anywhere in sight. It's a peculiar feeling knowing you are giving all you can to something, yet still have feelings of anxiety because it still doesn't feel it's enough. Combine that with the feelings of guilt that you have because you aren't spending enough time with your children or friends: loved ones who just want to spend a little time with you. The children have been left all weekend in someone else's care, in our case it was Serena's parents, who taking on the job of looking after many of the self-builders' children, giving up every weekend to enable us to continue building.

People would ask us about how things were going, and we all said it was all good and on schedule and everybody is still friends, which was true. However, until you do something like this you can't appreciate just how emotionally, mentally and physically draining it can be. We couldn't go anywhere without friends or family wanting to talk about the build, and you were never able to switch off. The attention was flattering, as was the support and encouragement, but there never was any other conversation. It becomes an obsession and takes over everything. I think it affected us all, plus the kids, which all sounds like a pretty bleak assessment of our great self-build project, but nothing ever worth doing is easy and this wasn't."

Life goes on, as they say. For the members of Broadhempston CLT, life was something that had become the necessity to finish the task that they had set out to do all those months ago, which now consumed every aspect of their lives. Ahead, they faced a winter of building without let-up:

13. Broadhempston

> "The days were starting to get shorter, which was slowing us down as the electricity was still in the running in process. No lighting meant limited work in the evenings, with the clocks going back the following Sunday.
> DECEMBER 2015.
> 19th December saw the usual workload, with the rare opportunity for us all to finish nice and early at 4:30, so we could get home and changed for the BCLT Christmas dinner at the Tally Ho Pub in Littlehempston. This had the added bonus of meeting Scott and Sophie's newborn son Kit, the newest addition to the team.
> We worked through the Christmas break, taking only a couple of days for the festivities, and concentrated on the plaster boarding as we wanted to stay ahead of the plasterers when they came in after the New Year."

Commander Geoff, as Gavin refers to him, had been very enterprising, attempting to arrange mutually-beneficial partnerships with local training providers. Although unsuccessful initially, they did manage to enlist the support of one local college and their carpentry course:

> "FEBRUARY 2016.
> The South Devon College carpentry department came to site and installed the staircase into plot 1, as well as the downstairs door frames to plot 2. They came back several times during the month to install the staircases in plots 2 and 3. Plots 4 and 5 were both partially completed."

The end of the actual build stage was now in sight, but there was still much to do before they could begin to enjoy the fruits of their arduous labours. The need to produce six individual family homes had to take second place to the necessity to complete the whole build for all, and the year-end financial round up was adding pressure to complete and sign off before further loan interest costs were incurred, so one final big push was needed:

> "APRIL 2016.
> Entering our 13th month of self building, you could sense the group were getting tired and, with houses getting close to a completion point, a bit keen to focus energy on working on individual houses to get ready for moving in. However, Commander Geoff gave us the news that for sign off we had to have certain jobs completed prior, as sign off was necessary to save us £5000 a month in loan interest. So the group were to concentrate all efforts on main project working rather than individual jobs.
> At this point we all had friends and family over for painting parties and hired some skilled labour for jobs like the tiling of floors to enable installing the bathrooms and kitchens to prevent more delays."

The six Broadhempston families were able to take up full occupancy of their homes later that summer and were fully signed-off by November 2016, but as you will see from their Facebook page it is very much an on-going effort. I am personally grateful to them all for agreeing to contribute their experiences to this book; plot 1 – Scott, Sophie and family, plot 2 – Gavin, Serena and family, plot 3 – Simon and Jośe, plot 4 – Hugo and Harriet, plot 5 – Andreas, Sarah and family, plot 6 – Commander Geoff, Sibylle and family. At the moment of my writing of this chapter, they were planting trees and adding their individual personalities to their homes. There is no doubt that what they have done for their families is quite incredible and the way that they have promoted their achievements is an inspiration to many others out there to try. They have very kindly offered to compile a guidance package (a concise 'how to' guide) for all those who are considering setting up a Community Land Trust self-build; they have gained considerable experience and insight and they wish to share that with others. Gavin summed up the whole incredible undertaking in these two paragraphs earlier in his account. These are words that could have been written in the 1950's, which show that the sense of elation and the building of not just homes, but actual communities, is a very worthwhile and rewarding endeavour and not having the skill is not a barrier to achieving the dream:

"It was amazing what had been achieved and the effort and time and just plain hard work that everyone had put in. We are basically a random bunch of people with very varied jobs, skills, attitudes and beliefs…

What we do have, is a shared passion for living in the place we all love and a drive to see this through, also a healthy respect for each other that comes from working so long together as a team; we also have unbelievable support from friends and family"

"Anyone who decides to take on a project like this, which means giving up your life as you know it, should really think hard about whether it is right for them and their family. However, the feeling you get from achieving the milestones of seeing something successfully completed counters the lows with massive highs that we all felt. I was over the moon the day my front door was put in, but felt great to see how happy Hugo was when we did the same for him. If I was asked if I would do it again? I know I would!!"

Figures 39 & 40 – The Broadhempston gang. The modern methods of quick-build.

*With grateful thanks to Broadhempston Community Land Trust for allowing me to publish these photographs.

Figures 41 & 42 – Straw bale construction. And now they have homes!

*With grateful thanks to Broadhempston Community Land Trust for allowing me to publish these photographs.

Chapter 14

Final Thoughts

Every history book that I write is a personal journey for me on so many different levels. First and foremost, it acts as a self-education; knowing very little about a topic ordinarily, I then set out to uncover as much research as possible, in order to illustrate in words the story that I narrate. My task is to commit that story to paper in some way in order to make it readable and comprehensible, and I would hope enjoyable and informative.

These final thoughts are in danger of being encapsulated in cliché but unfortunately, this is unavoidable as it is a truism that history is a circle; much of what has occurred before will inevitably repeat in some form or other. The self-help movement of the 1950's was born out of necessity after a raging World War that had left many urban centres in the United Kingdom severely bomb damaged. This, combined with the desire to clear inner cities of the pre-existing poverty, and shortages of everything including time, left many facing the only alternative open to them; building for themselves. Now this story has passed with one generation and out of memory. However, today we have a similar housing crisis, this time created from the lack of infrastructural investment over the last thirty years, combined with an over-heated and highly inflated housing market in many areas of the country. Those that are driven to build now are not doing so because they have learnt something from history, they are doing it because they have only one option left open; they have to build for themselves. I have no doubt that if we ever resolve our current housing needs and then develop a similar crisis a generation later, the same repetition of obscured history will occur again; this is the condition of history.

So much of what is written under the title of history can be dry and not easy to navigate your way through, either by the use of very exclusive language, or through the expectation that you may have prior knowledge of something that is being recounted. What I try to do in each book is offer the entire picture, so that there is very little background to have to know, or to have to have gained an understanding of previously. This can create some difficulty, especially with a topic that has inevitable links to a political time and the consequences of the political changes since. I did not set out to write a political book, nor do I claim any political affiliation, I have merely tried to put all of what happened into the context in which that 'happening' came into existence, and the various twists and turns subsequently. It is an unavoidable consequence that this topic would have a political frame, as differing ideologies view housing as either something that should be provided for all, equally, or that everyone should have the right to aspire to through whatever means possible.

Indeed, when I first explored this topic it was purely a personal journey of a story that was very close to my heart. Without my parents' determination and their 27 other neighbours, I do not think that I would have aspired to be the person that I am today. There is no doubt that my parents imparted that same self-determination that all things were possible with a great deal of hard work, to me, and my siblings. As a consequence, we have all carried that same drive through our own adult lives. They proved that there are no barriers to what you can do, only those that you place before yourself. I believe I speak for all of the offspring of the Silver Birch scheme, when I write that we are all truly grateful for what our parents did for us.

The same will be true for all of these modern pioneers, particularly those who will eventually grow up in the houses that their parents build in Community Land Trusts and the like. When you read both of the accounts given by Helen for St. Minver and Gavin for Broadhempston and know that there are potentially two hundred other groups making the same tremendous efforts to house their families through their own hard work and perspiration, I know that their children will be enormously proud when they become fully aware of just how amazing their parents have been, and that it is something out of the norm to actually build your own house, piece by piece. But there is more to this. A house built for one family is a fantastic achievement, however, when a committed group comes together and builds together, it is actually the building of a community. The children there grow up together, they share a common love and respect for their homes and their areas; it is a shared experience in every sense of the word.

For the many that built out of necessity in the 1950's there were some extremely hard years that followed those back-breaking efforts. As is clear one particular town, Solihull, benefited enormously. I am very proud to say that I come from Solihull, though I am often met with a certain scepticism as most assume those that come from such a town to be affluent and dare I say snobby. I am not a Silhillian by birth, but there is no doubt that I have benefited greatly from being able to grow up in such a location, with the access to the education that I had. None of that would have been possible for me unless Solihull had welcomed the self-help groups as they did, and more importantly, we were never stigmatised as families; we were absorbed as part of the community. I also believe that Solihull drew great benefits from housing so many via this route, for as these souls did build their own communities, it so follows that they were very law-abiding, socially aware groups of people; communities that had considerable respect and pride in the places that they lived. Any town or village that were to invest today in such a strategy would have the same responsible and respectable communities in their midst. In these days of ever-tightening council funding, less damage and vandalism to repair and greater self-care and investment in communal areas means less expenditure for a Local Authority. Community self-build has much to offer any enterprising Local Authority with the vision to actively promote and support this strategy. There is no doubt, it is personally one of the most fulfilling and rewarding experiences that you can go through, to build your own home.

One of the most interesting findings of this voyage, was that of how little is known about the notion of community self-build. Obviously, in the South West of England there is a very high-profile to this movement but very little knowledge or awareness elsewhere; even local authorities (or at least those that work in departments dealing with Freedom of Information requests) seem vague on the matter. It could be said with so many strategies and initiatives in place currently trying to address the housing shortfall that this praiseworthy strategy has become obscured. If that is the case, I do hope that this narrative will go some way towards raising the profile of this possibility. I would like this book to stand for all of those who have undertaken such an arduous and monumental task, past and present. All the

14. Final thoughts

thousands and thousands back in the decade of the 1950's and the many hundreds today who are in that process right now, this gargantuan effort needs recognition and praise. I opened the account with a speech from 1952 by Martin Lindsay MP, he called the self-help movement then 'the new Elizabethan's'. We have the same monarch today, and it is as true a statement now for our current crop of self-builders as it was back then.

I do not believe that any collective of people trying to live their normal complicated/busy lives with work and children, wake up one morning and decide to self-build. The people that become most determined to do so, have become so frustrated by their own housing circumstances and have again and again, gone through all possible other avenues before they finally resolve in desperation to follow this route. This is a course – as we know - that many admit they have no knowledge of, or skill in, but still they have experienced so many fruitless searches for a solution that this is the only positive way in which they can finally take control of their own destiny. It takes a lot of guts and hard work to take on a project like this, even more to be the initiator, and by far the biggest frustration at this stage is to find that you can go no further as there is simply no land available.

If we remember from the previous two chapters, St. Minver were fortunate that Dave Wills shared the same passion to save Rock as did Bill Dingle, and made plots of his land available to the trust at nominal values, in the same way that cousins by marriage offered their two-acre field at low value to assist the self-builders of Broadhempston. To view the interactive map on the Self-Build Portal and see it literally crammed with people seeking low-cost available plots for sale is quite astonishing. Either more councils have got to set aside land - brown field sites for instance - and create serviced plots (an access road, full drainage, and electricity taken to the site), or many more land owners have to follow a philanthropic route (maybe with a tax-relief incentive for losing a percentage of their land at a nominal value). The likelihood of the housing market de-valuing is slim and as long as it continues to rise astronomically it will become more and more unaffordable to local people, especially in areas of high tourism.

There is a tipping point of course. After all, these more affluent 'outcomers' that move to the touristic parts of the United Kingdom still require all of the normal infrastructural services and shops etcetera. If local young people can no longer afford to exist on local normal income, they will move away; they will have to. This will have an inevitable impact on these villages and towns, as they will eventually lose their shops and out-of-town attractions. Of course, this will no longer attract the high-rollers who like the convenience of having it all on their doorstep, but that may well rebalance the local house pricing structure. However, that would take decades to play out and the problems are right now, at this moment. It requires a vision on a national scale to resolve our housing problems, meanwhile, as long as land can be made available in some small way, there will always be those groups of frustrated young people who will take action, and after years of struggle they will seek to <u>'build their dream'</u>.

Bibliography

Books

ALLPORT, A. (2009) *Demobbed-Coming home after the Second World War* 1st Ed. (Kindle) Yale: Yale University Press

BLANCHET, E. (2014) *Prefab Homes.* 1st Ed. (Kindle) Oxford: Shire

DEBNEY, J. (2011) *The Dangerfields: Munitions and Memories.* 1st Ed. Warwickshire: Brewin

DEBNEY, J. (2018) *Far Away Hills* 1st Ed. (Kindle) Amazon KDP

KYNASTON, D. (2007) *Austerity Britain* 1st Ed. (Kindle) London: Bloomsbury

LOWE, S. (2011) *The Housing Debate.* 1st Ed. (Kindle) Bristol: policy Press

MERRETT, S. (1979) *Stae Housing in Britain* 1st Ed. London: Routledge

RAVETZ, A. (2001) *Council Housing and Culture-The History of a Social Experiment.* 1st Ed. (Kindle) London: Routledge.

SKIDELSKY, R. (2014) *Britain since 1900-A success story?* 1st Ed. (Kindle) London: Vintage

Unpublished Texts

DAVIES, P. (2005) *The Shakespeare Housing Association*-Solihull Central Library

GROGAN, R. (2009) *"We built with Fortitude" Recollections of a Self –Help Housing Association*-Solihull Central Library

HISCOX, W. C. (2003) *Solihull Progressive Housing Association Ltd-(Self-Help Housing Association)*-Solihull Central Library

Solihull Urban District Council Minutes

8/7/46 (Housing Committee) 1. Control of Civil Building
8/7/46 (Housing Committee) (C) Housing-supply of Building Materials and Components
8/7/46 (Public Works Committee) 2. Private Streets
4/12/46 (Public Works Committee) (a) Sheldon Area-Roads, Footpaths and Lighting
5/2/47 (Public Works Committee) 3. Unadopted Roads
5/3/47 (Housing Committee) (f) Housing Programme, 1947
2/4/47 (Housing Committee) (c) Rover Company Ltd-Housing Association
4/6/47 (Housing Committee) 46. Housing Programme for 1947
2/7/47 (Housing Committee) 74. Rover Co. Ltd.-Proposed Housing Association
10/9/47 (Housing Committee) Aluminium Houses
8/10/47 (Housing Committee) 140. Rover Housing Association
2/5/50 (General Purposes Committee) 182. Proposed Charter of Incorporation
7/6/50 (Housing Committee) 7. Self-Built Housing Association-Lucas No. 2 Branch-British Legion
6/9/50 (Housing Committee) 60. Fortitude Housing Association
9/10/50 (Housing Committee) 107. Housing Allocation
6/12/50 (Housing Committee) Housing Allocation
6/12/50 (Housing Committee) Self Help Associations
2/4/51 (Building, Plans and Town Planning) 653. Fortitude Housing Association Approval
30/40/51 (Building, Plans and Town Planning) Silver Birch Housing Assoc. U-Build It Housing Assoc. Sparkhill Housing Assoc. Tyburn Housing Assoc. Approval

14. Final thoughts

4/7/51 (Housing Committee) 37. Housing of Key Workers-Rover Co.
4/9/51 (General Purpose Committee) 31. Charter of Incorporation
5/9/51 (Housing Committee) Housing Act, 1936-Housing Associations
3/10/51 (Housing Committee) 71. Provision of Houses for Rover Employees
7/11/51 (Housing Committee) 82. Housing Act, 1936-Housing Associations
7/11/51 (Housing (management) Sub-Committee) 76. (1) Building Licenses
5/12/51 (Housing Committee) 103. Self-Help Housing
5/12/51 (Housing Committee) 105. Provision of Houses for Rover Employees
9/1/52 (Housing Committee) 116. Housing Programme, 1952
9/1/52 (Housing Committee) Housing of Birmingham Residents
22/1/52 (Housing Committee) Housing Programme, 1952
22/1/52 (Minutes of the Council) (230) Housing Committee
6/2/52 (Housing Committee) 130. Housing Programme, 1952
6/2/52 (Housing Committee) 131. Self Help Housing Associations
2/4/52 (Housing Committee) 171. Tyburn Housing Association
2/4/52 (Housing Committee) 177. Shirley Self Build Housing Association
11/6/52 (Housing Committee) 10. Housing Associations and Self Help Groups: Contribution to Local Housing Needs
11/6/52 (Housing Committee) 25. Self-Help Housing Associations.
9/7/52 (Housing Committee) 29. Invicta Housing Association
9/7/52 (Housing Committee) 30. Progressive Housing Association
9/7/52 (Housing Committee) 31. Progressive Housing Association-Housing Act, 1936
9/7/52 (Housing Committee) 34. Shirley Self-Build Housing Association
9/7/52 (Housing Committee) 43. Self-Help Housing Associations
10/9/52 (Housing Committee) 51. The United Self Help Housing Association
10/9/52 (Housing Committee) 53. A.I.T. Housing Association Ltd.
10/9/52 (Housing Committee) 56. Allocation to Self Help Housing Associations
10/9/52 (Housing Committee) 57. Solihull Progressive Housing Association Ltd.
8/10/52 (Housing Committee) 84. Fortitude Housing Association-3rd Allocation
8/10/52 (Housing Committee) A.I.T. Housing Society Ltd.
7/1/53 (Housing Committee) 131. Cateswell Self-Build Housing Association
7/1/53 (Housing Committee) 139. Issue of Building Licences
4/2//53 (Housing Committee) 156 Supply of Bricks
4/3/53 (Housing Committee) 165. Self Help Housing Associations-Further Allocations
4/3/53 (Housing Committee) 183. Lump Sum Subsidy for Housing Associations
29/4/53 (Housing Committee) 206. Shakespeare Housing Association-Second Allocation
10/6/53 (Housing Committee) 6. Advance (Ex-Services) Housing Association Ltd.
10/6/53 (Housing Committee) 11. Silver Birch Housing Association
10/6/53 (Housing Committee) 12. Self-Help Housing Associations-Allocation
10/6/53 (Housing Committee) Sparkhill Housing Association-Fourth Allocation
10/6/53 (Housing Committee) 24. Row Wood Farm Housing Association
9/9/53 (Housing Committee) 53. United Effort Housing Association
9/9/53 (Housing Committee) 55. Lease of Land to Housing Associations
9/9/53 (Housing Committee) 56. Solihull Progressive Housing Association
9/9/53 (Housing Committee) 58. Silver Birch Housing Association

7/10/53 (Housing Committee) 81. Supreme Housing Association
7/10/53 (Housing Committee) 83. Housing Progress Report
7/10/53 (Housing Committee) 84. Lavender Hill Housing Association
4/11/53 (Housing Committee) 94. Shirley Self-Build Housing Ltd.
2/12/53 (Housing Committee) 124. Housing Progress Report
2/12/53 (Housing Committee) 134. Shakespeare Housing Association
4/3/54 (General Purposes Committee) Royal Charter of Incorporation granted
2/6/54 (Public Works Committee) 11. Private Street Works
8/12/54 (Housing Committee) 118. Self Help Housing Associations-Sale of Properties to Members
2/11/55 (Housing Committee) 98. Silverbirch (sic) Housing Association-Sale of Properties to Members
5/12/56 (Housing Committee) Self-Help Housing Associations
9/1/57 (Housing Committee) 145. Self-Help Housing Associations
2/4/58 (Housing Committee) 266. Lease of Land-Housing Associations

Academic Papers / Working Papers / Presentations
Birmingham University Housing and Communities Research Group-Co-operative Housing (2015) Working Paper http://www.birmingham.ac.uk/Documents/college-social-sciences/social-policy/IASS/housing/2015/working-paper-series/HCR-WP-1-2015.pdf

LLOYD, M. G., PEEL, D. & JANSSEN-JANSEN, L. B. (2015) Self-build in the UK and Netherlands: mainstreaming self-development to address housing shortages?, Urban, Planning and Transport Research, 3:1, 19-31, DOI: 10.1080/21650020.2014.987403

MOORE, T. & MULLINS, D. (2013) Scaling Up Or Going Viral? Comparing Self Help Housing and Community Land Trust Facilitation. PPT. St Andrews University-April 2013

MULLINS, D. (2009) Housing Scoping Paper-Self Help Housing Birmingham: TSRC

MURPHY, L. R. (1970) *"Rebuilding Britain: The government's Role in Housing and Town Planning, 1945-57"* Historian 32(3) pp. 410-427
http://housing-studies-association.org/wp-content/uploads/2013/10/Moore-HSA13.pdf

Newspaper Articles
28/4/45-Warwickshire County News-Sheldon Residents Do Not Resent The Rate Increase But They Do Want The Council To Take Over The Roads
3/1/53-Solihull and Warwickshire County News-Little Homes Are Going Up In Solihull
24/1/53-Solihull and Warwickshire County News-Solihull Housing: Proud Position
30/5/53-Solihull and Warwickshire County News-Residents Object To Council house Plan For Shirley
20/6/53-Solihull and Warwickshire County News-Shift Systems For Local Schools?
27/6/53-Solihull and Warwickshire County News-council houses? No, Says Shirley
27/6/53-Solihull and Warwickshire County News-Land For Housing Subject To Compulsory Purchase Order

18/7/53-Solihull and Warwickshire County News-"Gaffers Only" Taunt Resented
25/7/53-Solihull and Warwickshire County News-Houses For City Workers In Solihull? An "Unfair" Assumption
1/8/53-Solihull and Warwickshire County News-Housing Workers Resent 'Self-Help'
15/8/53-Solihull and Warwickshire County News-Charter Now Regarded As Certainty
26/9/53-Solihull and Warwickshire County News-Public Enquiry Into Shirley Housing Proposal
10/10/53-Solihull and Warwickshire County News-Borough Of Solihull To Be Born In May?
14/11/53-Solihull and Warwickshire County News-Solihull, Another City Suburb?
25/11/11-https://www.theguardian.com/money/2011/nov/25/self-build-go-dutch The Guardian-Self Build: Its Time To Go Dutch

1/2/15 http://www.birminghammail.co.uk/news/nostalgia/carl-chinn-birminghams-homelessness-timebomb-8545214 Birmingham Mail-Housing and Greedy Landlords Saw Families Forced Out On The Streets-Professor Carl Chinn

6/1/17-http://www.dailymail.co.uk/property/article-3938746/What-prefab-homes-cost-ones-build.html Looking for a quick way to build your own Grand Design? We look at striking modern prefab homes and what they cost

Acts, Cabinet Papers, Ministerial Papers, Speeches, government Websites
Cab. 45/226 Temporary Housing. 13.10.45
Cab. 51/43 The Building Industry and The Housing Programme
Cab. 52/216 A Property Owning Democracy
Cab. 53/219 White Paper on Housing Policy
Cab. 53/250 White Paper on Housing Policy
Communities and Local government (2008) Community Land Trusts-A Consultation. London: Department for Communities and Local government
http://researchbriefings.files.parliament.uk/documents/SN04903/SN04903.pdf
Communities and Local government (2017) Fixing Our Broken Housing Market. London: Department for Communities and Local government
https://www.gov.uk/government/uploads/system/uploads/attachment_data/file/590463/Fixing_our_broken_housing_market_-_accessible_version.pdf
Conservative Party Manifesto 1951-www.conservativemanifesto.com
Hansard. (1952) H.C. Deb. Vol. 496, Col. 1674-84 (29 February)
Hansard (2016) H.L. Col. 1199-1234 (8 March)
HLG 101/464 Private Enterprise: Self-Help schemes (1945)-National Archive
HLG 101/591 Federation of Housing Associations: Correspondence with Self-Help Groups (1952)
HLG 101/592 Federation of Housing Associations: Correspondence with Self-Help Groups (1952-1955)
Housing Act 1936. (26 Geo. 5. & 1 Edw. 8. CH. 51)
Housing and Regeneration Act 2008 C. 1
Housing Associations Act 1985 C. 69

H M government (2011) Laying The Foundations: A Housing Strategy For England
Homes and Communities Agency (2015 Custom Build Serviced Plots Loan Fund Prospectus-Continuous Market Engagement
Self-Build and Custom Housing Act 2015 C. 17
Social Policy Section (2013) Community Land Trusts. House of Commons Library
Town and Country Planning Act 1990 C. 106

Industry Led Papers
NASBA (2011) An Action Plan to Promote the Growth of Self Build Housing

Film Clips / Radio Interviews
Broadhempston CLT https://youtu.be/hBToqBnrUwM
Grand Designs-Hedgehog Housing Co-op Brighton https://youtu.be/VaB_7S8cQII
Legion Builders (1949) http://www.britishpathe.com/video/legion-builders/query/LAVENDER
Legion Builders (1949) https://youtu.be/ASGDqMP9FdE
WHITEHEAD, C. (LSE)-Radio 2-Jeremy Vine-Housing Crisis-7 February 2017
St. Minver Community Land Trust (2011) https://vimeo.com/23261958

Miscellaneous Websites and Links

1950's Context
http://www.birminghammail.co.uk/news/nostalgia/gallery/aerial-views-castle-vale-castle-7382951 Ariel Views of Bromford Lane
http://www.britainfromabove.org.uk/image/eaw008640?keyword=15403&view=list&ref=102 Ariel Views of Birmingham and Bromford Lane
http://www.epsomandewellhistoryexplorer.org.uk/MoreOnPrefabs.pdf Prefabs-the solution to the housing crisis
http://www.heritage-explorer.co.uk/web/he/searchdetail.aspx?id=4601&crit=prefab&start=1&rt=0 Prefabs-Wake Green Road, Birmingham
http://www.historyandpolicy.org/policy-papers/papers/the-hidden-history-of-housing Prefabs
https://think-left.org/2014/11/06/fifty-men-of-brum Think Left-Reproduction of Fifty Men of Brum
http://www.iwm.org.uk/collections/item/object/30084361 Uni Seco Prefab
www.self-built.uk Silver Birch Housing Association-Archive

Present Day Context
https://broadhempstonclt.com Broadhempston Community Land Trust
http://www.communitylandtrusts.org.uk/what-is-a-clt/why-clts Community Land Trusts
http://mycommunity.org.uk/wp-content/uploads/2016/09/Community-self-build-factsheet-formatted.pdf Community Self Build Fact Sheet

14. Final thoughts

http://www.gov.scot/Publications/2011/02/03132933/2 Housing for the 21st Century- Scottish government

https://www.gov.uk/government/news/60-million-boost-for-communities-affected-by-second-homeownership Press Release 2016-Gavin Barwell M.P.

https://www.gov.uk/government/speeches/community-land-trusts-conference Speech (2008) Community Land Trust Conference-Grant Shapps M.P.

https://www.gov.uk/government/uploads/system/uploads/attachment_data/file/593937/LiveTable209.xlsx Housing Development by Type-1969-2016

http://localselfbuildregister.co.uk Local Self Build Register

http://www.nacsba.org.uk/about-us National Custom & Self Build Association

https://www.parliament.uk/business/publications/research/key-issues-parliament-2015/social-protection/housing-supply-Housing supply in 2015-2020 : Key issues for the 2015 Parliament

http://webarchive.nationalarchives.gov.uk/20160105160709/http://www.ons.gov.uk/ons/dcp171776_422383.pdf National Archive-UK Population Analysis

https://www.ons.gov.uk/peoplepopulationandcommunity/housing/bulletins/housingaffordabilityinenglandandwales/1997to2016 Office of National Statistics-Housing Affordability

http://www.scotframe.co.uk Modern Prefab Solutions

http://www.selfbuildportal.org.uk/website-welcome-from-kevin-mccloud Self Build Portal

http://www.the-self-build-guide.co.uk/st-minver-community-land-trust.html St Minver Community Land Trust/..l

Please feel free to contact me if you would like any further information – Jean Debney
jldebney@yahoo.co.uk

Printed in Great Britain
by Amazon